The Routledge Pocket Guide to Medical Latin

The Routledge Pocket Guide to Medical Latin is a medical reference tool like no other, providing an easy-to-use, extensive guide to Latin words and phrases commonly used in medical settings.

Offering readers a treasury of over 4000 Latin words and phrases, over 900 abbreviations, and numerous tables with dozens of useful Latin terms and interesting quotations drawn from the field of medicine, this volume also encompasses the related fields of pharmacy, botany, dentistry, and the veterinary sciences. This book provides quick and accessible definitions and explanations of Latin words and phrases used in the medical world, as well as a helpful pronunciation guide. In addition, there is a section of miscellaneous entries that comprises useful information, including common Latin prepositions, prefixes, and particles. Included at the end of this book is an extensive English-Latin index.

The Routledge Pocket Guide to Medical Latin is an invaluable reference work for medical and pharmacy students and practitioners, as well as general readers interested in the history of medicine and in medical terminology.

Dr. Jon R. Stone is a best-selling author and Professor of Religious Studies at California State University, Long Beach. He is the author of *Latin for the Illiterati*, *More Latin for the Illiterati*, *The Routledge Dictionary of Latin Quotations*, and *The Routledge Book of World Proverbs*, among many others.

The Routledge Latin Pocket Guides (in Three Separate Volumes)

Volume 1: *The Routledge Pocket Guide to Medical Latin*
Volume 2: *The Routledge Pocket Guide to Legal Latin*
Volume 3: *The Routledge Pocket Guide to Religious Latin*

Also by Jon R. Stone

Dictionnaire Rose des Locutions Latines (2007)
Latin for the Illiterati, 2nd ed. (2009)
More Latin for the Illiterati (1999)
The Routledge Book of World Proverbs (2006)
The Routledge Dictionary of Latin Quotations (2005)

and

The Craft of Religious Studies (1998)
The Essential Max Müller: On Language, Mythology, and Religion (2002)
Expecting Armageddon: Essential Readings in Failed Prophecy (2000)
A Guide to the End of the World (1993)
On the Boundaries of American Evangelicalism (1997)

The Routledge Pocket Guide to Medical Latin

Jon R. Stone

Routledge
Taylor & Francis Group
LONDON AND NEW YORK

Designed cover image: Brian Jackson/Alamy Stock Photo

First published 2024
by Routledge
4 Park Square, Milton Park, Abingdon, Oxon OX14 4RN

and by Routledge
605 Third Avenue, New York, NY 10158

Routledge is an imprint of the Taylor & Francis Group, an informa business

British Library Cataloguing-in-Publication Data
A catalogue record for this book is available from the British Library

Library of Congress Cataloging-in-Publication Data
Names: Stone, Jon R., 1959– author.
Title: The Routledge pocket guide to medical Latin / Jon R. Stone.
Description: Abingdon, Oxon ; New York, NY : Routledge, 2024. | Includes bibliographical references and index.
Identifiers: LCCN 2023044767 (print) | LCCN 2023044768 (ebook) | ISBN 9781032186061 (hbk) | ISBN 9781032186054 (pbk) | ISBN 9781003255352 (ebk)
Subjects: LCSH: Latin language—Terms and phrases. | Latin language—Medical Latin. | Medicine—Terminology.
Classification: LCC PA2387 .S76 2024 (print) | LCC PA2387 (ebook) | DDC 478.2/421—dc23/eng/20240201
LC record available at https://lccn.loc.gov/2023044767
LC ebook record available at https://lccn.loc.gov/2023044768

ISBN: 978-1-032-18606-1 (hbk)
ISBN: 978-1-032-18605-4 (pbk)
ISBN: 978-1-003-25535-2 (ebk)

DOI: 10.4324/9781003255352

Typeset in Times New Roman
by Apex CoVantage, LLC

For my sister-in-law

Dr. Dawn Salpaka Stone

with love and admiration

Ubi desinit philosophus, ibi incipit medicus.

(Where the philosopher ends, the physician begins.)

Contents

Preface

In the 1906 Introduction to Reginald Bennett's *Medical and Pharmaceutical Latin*, Henry Greenish of the Pharmaceutical Society of Great Britain lamented the noticeable shift away from the use of Latin in the writing of prescriptions both in Britain and on the Continent. While it seemed understandable that busy professionals would write their medical directives in the vernacular, 'yet,' as Greenish asserted, 'there is much to be said in favor of a universal language for pharmacopoeias and physicians' prescriptions.' For one thing, he argued, with the rapid advance in travel across Europe, let alone the globe, there would be every danger of inaccuracies in dispensing medicines and preparations written in a variety of languages. Such mishaps could be averted 'in the writing of these prescriptions in a universal language, Latin, by which they would be readily intelligible to the pharmacists of the countries, just as systematic descriptions of plants are written in Latin and are universally intelligible to systematic botanists' (1906:v).

It was to correct this deficiency that Bennett published his book, whose chief aim was to provide guidance to medical students whose modest familiarity with classical Latin might prove insufficient to meet the technical demands of the profession. Or, as Bennett himself put it, the medical student must learn 'to write correctly and to translate intelligibly and appropriately medical directions' as well as 'a large number of new prescriptions written in the abbreviated Latin style used by physicians' (1906:vii).

A decade later, in 1917, Otto Wall of the St. Louis College of Medicine echoed much of Bennett's and Greenish's concerns over the need for a common language in medicine. In the United States, however, Wall noted that vernacular English varied greatly by region—itself a cause for general confusion—and therefore made use of Latin as a common language among pharmacists and physicians all the more critical to know.

But further, Wall argued that the use of English by physicians might, first, 'needlessly hamper treatment of disease by the foolish notions of the patient' and, second, might arouse suspicions among the public who

> would soon know not only the nature of the ingredients of a prescription, but also their intrinsic values, and would, therefore,

> refuse to pay more than commercial profits for medical treatment or medicines, and proper remuneration for professional services and responsibilities would cease (1917:88).

Despite these financial concerns, and the ever-present carnival side-show of quacks and charlatans purveying their own nostrums—and the potential perils that lay in what Bennett had derisively dubbed 'self-drugging' among the masses—Wall voiced additional and more urgent concern over maintaining the professional standing of the healing arts in America, a standing that Latin as 'a universal language of science' had historically provided in Europe (1917:88–9; and Bennett 1906:viii).

Now, over a century later, the use of Latin as well as Greek words and phrases remains a common and necessary part of the specialized nomenclature that defines the epistemological foundations of the profession of medicine, not to mention law and theology. What those within these professions know about their respective fields—and how they know what they know—are questions that not only engage professors and practitioners but all college and graduate students who are preparing for careers in these fields, especially those in medicine.

Even so, it is not simply through the wealth of Greek and Latin words and phrases, prefixes and suffixes, that the modern world's connection to its classical past has been maintained. The body of knowledge bequeathed to medicine extends, as well, to the methods and techniques, prognosis and diagnosis, preparations and cures passed down and refined throughout the long centuries of development of the healing arts in Europe, America, and the West (and now being augmented by the healing wisdom of India and China). Indeed, much of the early techniques of medicine began during the Golden Age of Greece through the life and work of Hippocrates of Kos (BCE c.460–c.370) and passed along to the Roman world through the work of Galen (129–216 CE), and by many others.

It is primarily through the writings of Hippocrates, the natural philosopher and spiritual descendant of Asclepius, the god of medicine, that we find the earliest testament to the ancient art of healing, brought vividly to life through writings that display his inquisitive nature, reasoned process, and holistic approach. And it is to Hippocrates that the medical profession owes its method of careful empirical observation. For, as Elias Marks had long ago observed, it was Hippocrates who

> first divided diseases into *epidemic*, *endemic*, and *sporadic*, according to the present acceptations of these terms; and these diseases

> he again divided into *acute* and *chronic*. The duration of an acute disease was distinguished by the *beginning*, *height*, *decline*, and *termination* (1818:xxiii).

Although widely celebrated in his own time, Hippocrates is best known in our day for his popular maxim *primus non nocere*, the *first* duty of the physician is to *do no harm*, and for the Hippocratic Oath, in which young apprentices vowed to treat the sick, to abstain from causing intentional harm, and to keep the patient's confidence. Lesser known by the public is Hippocrates' book, *Aphorisms*, in which he laid out his careful observations of physical symptoms, prescribed treatments as well as noted their affects through short, memorable statements, much in the same way that a teacher might instruct his or her students. The most noteworthy of these statements, and perhaps the most quoted line from this collection, is found in the first of Hippocrates' aphorisms: '*Vita brevis, ars longa*' (Life is short, art long). Those who typically encounter this quote often see it emblazoned on car bumpers or stenciled on a sporty tee or as a webpage banner or on a refrigerator magnet. Though certainly a familiar saying today, the word *ars*, as translated from the Greek (τέχνη) and as also found in the Oath (line 10), actually means something like method, skill, trade, or possibly practice, not our modern concept of the fine arts, as in painting, sculpture, or dance. Most often this pithy statement strikes people as a deep or otherwise sober-minded saying, with the emphasis being on *vita brevis*. But in fact, Hippocrates' first aphorism, from which this line is plucked, conveys an even greater sense of urgency to those who wish to engage in the healing arts. In Latin: '*Vita brevis, ars longa, occasio praeceps, experientia fallax, judicium difficile.*' That is, 'Life is short, the art long; occasion fleeting; experience deceiving; judgment difficult.' And what doctor, nurse, or other medical practitioner has *not* felt this way? As Hippocrates himself might have counseled: Life is short, and the time that it requires to master the skills and techniques of medicine is longer than one life. Or, rather, life is short, learn all you can!

While originally formulated in the now-dead languages of Greek and Latin, over many generations since the time of the ancients, the methods and techniques of the art of medicine have continued to be sharpened, refined, and improved by their devoted heirs who also continued to employ Greek and Latin as their common specialized languages, thus giving sustained life and relevance to these classical languages into our own day. In this spirit, *The Routledge Pocket Guide to Medical Latin* offers readers a treasury of useful Latin words and phrases drawn from the field of medicine, broadly conceived to encompass the related branches of pharmacy, chemistry, botany, dentistry, and the veterinary sciences. (Persons involved in homeopathy, home remedies, and herbal cures may find these pages of interest as well.) Though written primarily as a quick reference for the student and practitioner of medicine, translations from Latin into English have been simplified wherever possible, and numerous examples have been provided to help clarify meanings that might otherwise appear vague or overly technical for general-interest readers. Obsolete terms and their related practices—such as bloodletting (*venaesectio*) and the use of leeches (*applicentur hirudines*)—have been included for historical interest.

In all, there are over 4000 separate entries in the main body of this guide with an additional 900 abbreviations of terms, instruments, elements, and medical directives. To help enliven this work, there is also included some 100 Latin maxims and quotations related to life, death, sickness, and the healing arts, including five by or attributed to Hippocrates himself. In addition, there is a section of miscellaneous entries that comprises a variety of useful reference information, from common Latin prepositions, particles, and prefixes, to the Roman calendar (months and days), a chart of Roman numerals, apothecary weights and measures, some Latin elements on the Periodic Table, and a veritable rainbow of Latin names for primary and secondary colors, and also a selection of Latin place names used both in medicine and by botanists. Included at the end of this book is an extensive, though not comprehensive, English-Latin Index.

To modify an old Spanish proverb: 'The silent err not.' To write a book, especially a reference book, often means that one risks making slips of the pen, in this case the inadvertent typographical error or awkwardly translated (or retranslated) word or phrase. And indeed, variations in spelling and word order as well as changes in meaning and usage over time can create their own challenges, hence my use of some older sources. In all of these instances, the author begs the reader's kind indulgence.

To write a book is also to incur debts, both professional as well as personal. Over the years, a number of university colleagues, program directors and chairs, professional associates, and editors have taken an interest in my Latin projects and also have pointed my career in the right direction. I owe them much and truly appreciate all their collegiality and support. Most especially, I would like to thank the editors and production staff at Routledge for nearly thirty years of fruitful association, with appreciation to the present efforts of Amy Davis-Pointer, Marcia Adams, Lizzi Rich, Sophie Dixon-Dash, Marie Roberts (Apex), and two unnamed reviewers for their guidance and helpful suggestions on how to improve this present volume.

Finally, my deepest gratitude always and forever goes to my family and longtime friends—far too many to name but not too many to remember with heartfelt appreciation. It seems more than fitting that the dedication of this pocket guide to medical Latin be presented to my sister-in-law, Dr. Dawn Salpaka Stone, my brother Richard's wife, whose whole life of dedicated service to the medical profession and joy-filled spirit inspire all who know her, me most of all.

Vita Brevis, Ars Longa

Jon R. Stone, Ph.D.
California State University, Long Beach
August 2023

References & Sources

Antoniou, George A., Stavros A. Antoniou, George S. Georgiadis, and Athanasios I. Antoniou. "A Contemporary Perspective of the First Aphorism of Hippocrates." *Journal of Vascular Surgery* 56, 3 (September 2012): 866–8.

Barton, Wilfred M., and Walter A. Wells. *Thesaurus of Medical Words and Phrases*. Philadelphia and London: W.B. Saunders & Co., 1903.

Bennett, Charles E. *New Latin Grammar* (2nd ed., revised; reprinted). Boston: Allyn and Bacon, 1963.

Bennett, Reginald R. *Medical and Pharmaceutical Latin for Students of Pharmacy and Medicine*. London: J. & A. Churchill, 1906.

Boardman, John, et al. (eds.). *The Oxford History of the Classical World*. New York: Oxford University Press, 1986.

Caspari, Charles, and E.F. Kelly. *A Treatise on Pharmacy for Students and Pharmacists* (7th ed., thoroughly revised). Philadelphia and New York: Lea & Febiger, 1926.

de Vaan, Michiel. *Etymological Dictionary of Latin and the Other Italic Languages*. Leiden and Boston: Brill, 2008.

Eggleston, Cary. *Essentials of Prescription Writing* (7th ed., revised). Philadelphia and London: W.B. Saunders Co., 1942.

French, Roger. *Canonical Medicine: Gentile da Foligno and Scholasticism*. Leiden and Boston: Brill, 2001.

Glare, P.G.W. (ed.). *Oxford Latin Dictionary* (2nd ed., reprinted with corrections). Oxford: Oxford University Press, 2016.

Gledhill, David. *The Names of Plants* (3rd ed.). Cambridge: Cambridge University Press, 2002.

Grant, Edward. *A History of Natural Philosophy from the Ancient World to the Nineteenth Century*. New York: Cambridge University Press, 2007.

Greene, Ryland W. *Lippincott's Medical Dictionary* (rev. ed.). Philadelphia: J.B. Lippincott Company, 1905.

Greenough, J.B., et al. (eds.). *Allen & Greenough's New Latin Grammar* (reprint of 1903 ed.). New Rochelle: Aristide D. Caratzas, 1983.

Guterman, Norbert (ed.). *The Anchor Book of Latin Quotations*. New York: Anchor Books, 1990.

Hippocrates. *Collected Works* (vol. 1, W.H.S. Jones, trans.). The Loeb Classical Library. London: William Heinemann; Cambridge: Harvard University Press, 1957.

Hoerr, Normand L., and Arthur Osol (eds.). *Blakiston's New Gould Medical Dictionary* (2nd ed.). New York: McGraw Hill Book Company, 1956.

Howe, George, and John Grover Beard. *Latin for Pharmacists*. Philadelphia: P. Blakiston's Son & Company, 1916.

Ince, Joseph. *The Latin Grammar of Pharmacy for Use of Medical and Pharmaceutical Students* (10th ed.). London: Baillière, Tindall & Cox, 1920.
Israelowich, Ido. *Patients and Healers in the High Roman Empire*. Baltimore: Johns Hopkins University Press, 2015.
Konstantinidis, Giannis. *Elsevier's Dictionary of Medicine and Biology* (Part 1, Basic Table). San Diego: Elsevier, 2005.
Lewis, Charlton T., and Charles Short. *A New Latin Dictionary* (revised, enlarged, and rewritten). New York: Harper & Brothers; Oxford: The Clarendon Press, 1884.
Marks, Elias. *The Aphorisms of Hippocrates, etc.* New York: Collins & Company, 1818.
McKeown, J.C. *A Cabinet of Ancient Medical Curiosities*. New York: Oxford University Press, 2017.
Moreland, Floyd L., and Rita M. Fleischer. *Latin: An Intensive Course*. Berkeley: University of California Press, 1977.
Morwood, James. *A Latin Grammar*. Oxford and New York: Oxford University Press, 1999.
Muldoon, Hugh C. *Lessons in Pharmaceutical Latin and Prescription Writing and Interpretation* (3rd ed., revised). New York: John Wiley & Sons, 1937.
Riley, H.T. (ed.). *Dictionary of Latin Quotations, etc.* London: Henry G. Bohn, 1859.
Scanlon, Valerie C. *Essentials of Anatomy and Physiology* (5th ed.). Philadelphia: F.A. Davis Company, 2007.
Scott, William A. "The Practice of Medicine in Ancient Rome." *Canadian Anaesthetists' Society Journal* 2, 3 (July 1955): 281–90.
Simpson, D.P. *Cassell's Latin-English/English-Latin Dictionary* (5th ed.). New York: Macmillan Publishing Company, 1977.
Stearn, William T. *Botanical Latin* (3rd ed.). Newton Abbot and London: David & Charles Publishers, 1983.
Stone, Jon R. *More Latin for the Illiterati*. New York and London: Routledge, 1999.
Stone, Jon R. *The Routledge Dictionary of Latin Quotations*. New York and London: Routledge, 2005.
Stone, Jon R. *Latin for the Illiterati* (2nd ed.). New York and London: Routledge, 2009.
Thomas, J. *A Comprehensive Medical Dictionary, etc.* Philadelphia: J.B. Lippincott & Company, 1876.
Trayner, John. *Latin Phrases and Maxims*. Edinburgh: William Patterson, 1861.
Wall, Otto A. *The Prescription, Therapeutically, Pharmaceutically, Grammatically and Historically Considered* (4th ed., revised). St. Louis: C.V. Mosby Company, 1917.
Webster's II: New Riverside University Dictionary. Boston: Houghton Mifflin Company, 1984.

Webster's New World Dictionary (3rd College ed.). New York: Prentice Hall, 1988.

Wheelock, Frederic M., and Richard A. LaFleur. *Wheelock's Latin* (6th ed., revised). New York: HarperCollins, 2005.

Woods, Robert S. *The Naturalist's Lexicon*. Pasadena: Abbey Garden Press, 1944.

Wyeth, John. *An Epitome of Therapeutics*. Philadelphia: John Wyeth & Brothers, 1901.

Yapijakis, Christos. "Hippocrates of Kos, the Father of Clinical Medicine, and Asclepiades of Bithynia, the Father of Molecular Medicine." *In Vivo* 23 (2009): 507–14.

Pronunciation Guide

In pronouncing Latin, it is helpful to know that most Latin sounds have corresponding standard American English sounds, but with the rules for long and short vowel sounds being more consistently applied. Indeed, long and short vowel sounds refer simply to the duration of the sound, that is, how long the vowel should be voiced within its given syllable. For convenience, the basic Latin vowel sounds are pronounced accordingly: **a** = ah, **e** = eh, **i** = ee, **o** = oh, **u** = oo.

As examples, the long *a* in *father* is the same sound as the long *a* in the Latin word *pater*. The short *a* in the English words *par* and *far* are very similar in sound to that of the Latin words *pax* and *fax*. The short *e* in *pet* is similar in sound to the Latin *et*, as is the short *i* in *twig* the same as the *i* in the Latin word *signum*. The long *o* in *Ohio* sounds very much like the *o* in the Latin word *dolor*. Similarly, the short *o* in *pot* is pronounced similarly to the short *o* in *populus*. Likewise, the Latin *u* in *runa* and *pudicus*, one long and the other short, sound the same as the long and short *u* vowels in *rude* and *put*.

Readers should also keep in mind that in Latin, unlike English, all the syllables in a word are pronounced, including the final *e* and *es*, such as in the words *arte* and *artes*, *duce* and *duces*, *fide* and *fides*, *opinione*, and *legiones*.

With respect to Latin consonants, one should nearly always pronounce them as those in standard American English (e.g., **b** = b, **d** = d, **f** = f, **l** = l, **m** = m, **n** = n, **p** = p, **r** = r, **s** = s, **t** = t, *etc.*), with the exception of **c**, **g**, **h**, and **v**, which are always pronounced like **k** (as in kirk), **g** (as in give, gave, and go), **h** (as in hard), and **v** as **v** or **w** (as in vine and vise or we and was) respectively. The letters **i** and **j**, when placed before another vowel, such as *iam*/*jam* and *ius*/*jus*, are pronounced like the consonant **y** (as in you, yam, and yeti), not the consonant **j**. The convention of substituting the letter **j** for **i**, when used as a consonant, appeared after the Classical period. For the sake of simplicity, both **i** and **j** are used here.

Lastly, with respect to vowel diphthongs, most Classical Latin linguists prefer to pronounce them as follows: **ae** as if it were a long *i* (as in pine); **oe** as *oi* (as in boy); **au** as *ou* or *ow* (as in bough or now);

ei as a long *a* (as in weight); **eu** as *eu* (as in feud); and **ui** as *wee* (as in the French *oui*).

For further discussion, guidelines, and helpful examples, please consult LaFleur's *Wheelock's Latin* (6th ed.), *Allen & Greenough's New Latin Grammar*, Bennett's *New Latin Grammar*, and Morwood's *A Latin Grammar*.

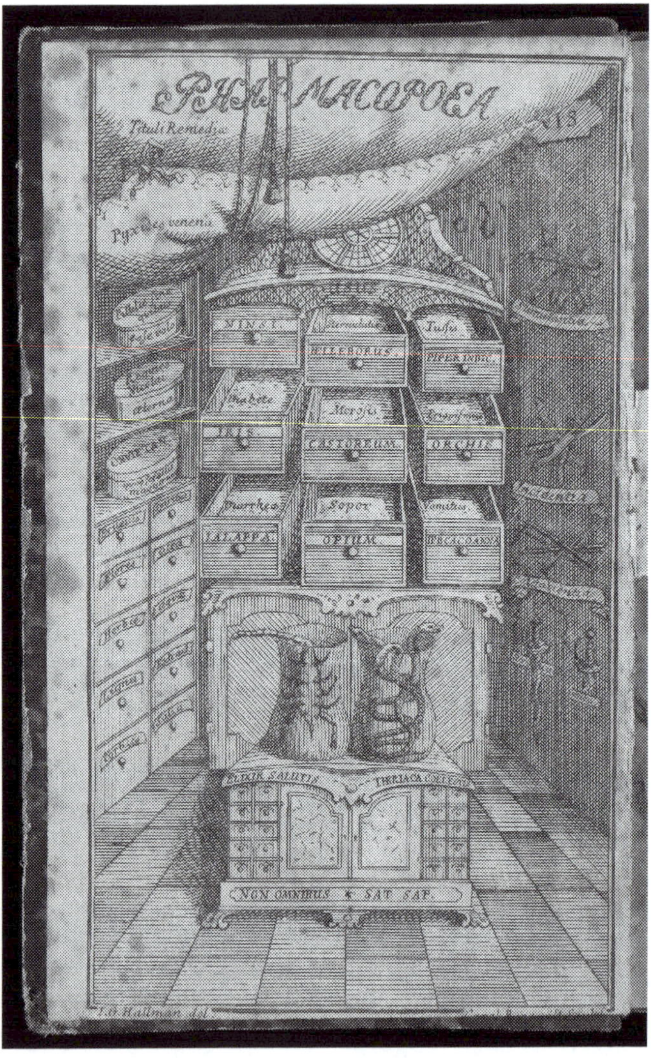

PHARMACOPOEA
Tituli Remedia
Tussis
HELLEBORUS
Mersis
CASTOREUM
ORCHIS
Sopor
OPIUM
NON OMNIBUS ✠ SAT SAP

The Routledge Pocket Guide to Medical Latin

A

a balineo: after bathing
a capite ad calcem: from head to heel (i.e., from top to bottom)
a datu: from the date
a dextra: on the right
a die: from that day or date
a latere: from the side
a primo: from the first
a sinistra: on the left
a solis ortu usque ad occasum: from sunrise to sunset
a tergo [in the rear]: behind; from behind
ab extra [from without]: from the outside
ab incunabulis [from the cradle]: from childhood
ab initio: from the beginning; from the start
ab intra [from within]: from the inside
ab invito: unwillingly; against one's will
ab parvulis: from childhood
abhinc: hereafter; from here on
abies: fir tree
ablutio: washing away; cleansing
abrasus: scraped off; close shaven
absens: absent
absente febre (**abs. febr.**): in the absence of fever
absinthium: absinth; wormwood
absolutus: absolute
absorbens: absorbent
abortus: aborted; prematurely born
abusque ulla nota: without any mark
acacia or **acaciae gummi**: gum arabic
acanthulus: an instrument for removing thorns, splinters, and the like from wounds
acanthus: having thorns or spines; the acanthus plant
acaulis: having no stem or stalk; stemless
acephalus: without a head; headless

DOI: 10.4324/9781003255352-1

acer [sharp]: a needle
acerbitas: acidity; sourness
acerbus (acerb.): sour; bitter
acetas: an acetate
acetica: preparations of vinegar
aceticus: acetic
acetonum: acetone
acetum (acet.): vinegar
acetum Britannicum: aromatic vinegar
acetum rutaceum: vinegar of rue
aciditas: acidity
aciditate infestante: when troubled with acidity
acidulus: sourness
acidum or **acidus**: acid; sharp; sour in taste
acidum aereum: an older name for carbon dioxide
acidum hydrochloricum: hydrochloric acid (earlier names include *acidum muriaticum* and *acidum salis*)
acidum lacticum: lactic acid
acidum sulfuricum or **acidum sulphuricum**: sulfuric acid
acidum tannicum: tannic acid
acinus: a berry; the seed of a berry
acme: highest point; the peak (e.g., the height of a fever or a disease)
acne rosacea or **rosacea**: acne (see also, **gutta rosea**)
aconitum: monk's hood; sometimes monk's head (a strong poison)
aconitum napellus: wolfsbane (a strong poison)
acor: acidity (e.g., in the stomach)
activatus: activated
actus: act
acuminatus: pointed
aculeatus: having a stinger or barb
aculeus: a sting; a stinger
acus: a needle
acutifolius: having pointed leaves
acutus: sharp; accute
ad: to; at; up to
ad alvum excitandum (ad alv. excitand.): to stimulate the bowels
ad aptam crassitudinem (ad apt. crass.): to a suitable thickness or consistency
ad conciliandum gustum: to suit the taste; with consideration to the palate
ad defectionem animi (ad def. animi): to fainting

ad deliquium (**ad deliq.**): to fainting
ad duas vices (**ad duas vic.** or **ad 2 vic.**): at two times; in two doses
ad gratam aciditatem (**ad grat. acid.**): to an agreeable sourness
ad gustum: to taste; according to taste
ad gustum conciliandum: to suit the taste; with consideration to the palate
ad hoc: to the moment; for this purpose
ad libitum (**ad lib.**): at will
ad partes dolentes (**ad part. dol.**): to the painful parts
ad plenum: fully; copiously; to the brim
ad recidivum praecavendum (**ad recid. praec.**): to prevent a relapse
ad saturandum (**ad sat.**): to saturation
ad secundum vicem (**ad sec. vic.** or **ad 2nd vic.**): for the second time
ad syrupi densitatem evaporet: let it evaporate to a syrupy consistence
ad tempus [at the right time]: in due time; according to the circumstances
ad tertiam vicem (**ad ter. vic.**): for the third time
ad tres alias vices (**ad 3 al. vic.**): at three other times; for three other times
ad tres vices (**ad 3 vic.**): at three times; for three times
ad unum: to the one; without exception
ad unum omnes: all to the one; unanimously
ad usum externum (**ad us. ext.**): for external use
ad vivum [to the life]: lifelike
ad vomitum sedandum: to allay vomiting
adde (**ad.** or **add.**): let there be added
addendus (**addend.**): to be added
additum (pl. **addita**): something added
adeps: lard; fat
adeps auserinus: goose grease
adeps depuratus: purified lard
adeps gadi: cod liver oil
adeps lanae: wool fat; lanolin
adeps ovillus: mutton suet
adeps salis expers: salt-free lard
adeps sine sale: lard without salt
adeps suillus: hog's lard
adhaesivus: adhesive
adhibendus (**adhib.** or **adhibend.**): to be used; to be applied
adhuc: while; as yet
adjuvans: helping; assisting; an adjuvant (i.e., a strengthening agent that assists other remedies)

adlevare or **adlevatio**: to alleviate; alleviating
adligare or **adligo**: to bind up [a wound]
admove (admov.): apply
admoveatur (admov.): let it be applied
adolescens: youth
adsto: to be present
adstans: present
adstante febre (adst. febr.): in the presence of fever
adstrictus: tight; confined
adstringens: astringent
adsum: to be present
adultus: an adult
adustus: burnt; singed; also, sunburnt
adversum or **adversus (adv.)**: against
aeger (f. **aegra; aeg.**): sick; the patient; a medical excuse
aegri somnia [a sick person's dreams]: hallucinations
aegrota: a sick woman
aegrotat (pl. **aegrotant**) [he or she is ill]: a medical excuse
aegrotus: a sick man
aequalis (aeq.): equal
aer: air
aeratus: made of or covered with bronze; aerated
aerugo: verdigris (i.e., a copper patina)
aes: copper or brass
aestivus: pertaining to summer; summerlike; summery
aestuarium: a vapor bath
aestus: heat
aetas: age
aether: ether
aethyl: ethyl
aethylenum: ethylene
aethereus: ethereal
aethusa cynapium: garden hemlock (or fool's parsley)
affectus: affected
affinis: having affinity with
affluxus: flowing to
agaricus: a mushroom
aggrediente febre (aggred. febr.): on the approach of fever
aggressus: an attack
aggressus febris: an attack of fever

agita (**agit.**): shake
agita ante dispensationem: shake before dispensing
agita ante sumendum: shake before taking
agitando: by shaking
agitando miscentur: let them be mixed by shaking
agitato vase (**agit. vas.**): the vial being shaken
agitatus: having been shaken
agrestis: pertaining to the field; wild
ala [wing]: the armpit (see also, **axilla**)
ala dextra: the right wing or armpit
ala laeva: the left wing or armpit
alatus: having wings; winged
alba et atra: white and black
albus (**alb.**): white
alcohol: alcohol
alcohol absolutum: absolute alcohol
alcoholicus: alcoholic
alga: seaweed
alimentum: food
aliquot: some; a few
alius alias: one now, another later
alkalinus: alkaline
alkaloidum: alkaloid
allevare or **adlevare**: to alleviate
alligare or **adligare**: to bind
allium or **alium**: garlic; garlic plant (properly, **allium sativum**)
allium cepa: onion; onion plant (see also, **cepa**)
alnus: the alder
aloe: aloe plant
alpinia nutans: false cardamom
alter: the other
alter . . . alter . . . (**alt. . . . alt. . . .**): the one . . . and the other . . .
alter ego: a second self
alternis annis (**alt. anni.**): every other year
alternis diebus (**alt. die.**): every other day
alternis horis (**alt. hor.**): every other hour
alternus: alternate; one after the other
alterum tantum [as much again]: twice as much
althaea: marsh mallow plant
alumen: alum

aluta: leather
alutam mollens: upon soft leather
alvearium: the external opening of the ear
alveolus: a little hollow; a tray or trough
alveus: hollow area; cavity
alviducus or **alviducum**: a laxative
alvo adstricta (**alv. adst.**): the bowels being constricted (i.e., constipated)
alvo laxata (**alv. laxat.**): the bowels being relaxed
alvo soluta: with the bowels being loosened
alvus: the bowels
amabilis: able to be loved; lovable
amarities: bitterness
amarus: bitter
ambiguus: ambiguous; going two ways; uncertain
ambo [two together]: both
ambrosia [food of the gods]: an antidote to poison and deadly toxins
amens: insane
amiantus: asbestos
amictus: cloaked; clothed
ammonia: ammonia
ammoniatus: ammoniated
amor: love
amphetamina: amphetamine
amphora: a jar
amplus (**amp.**): large; ample
ampulla: a small bottle
amygdala: almond
amygdala amara: bitter almond
amygdala dulcis: sweet almond
amygdalae: the tonsils
amygdalus persica: a peach
amylaceus: of starch
amylum: starch
ana (**aa** or **āā**): of each
analgesicus: an analgesic
androgynus: an androgyne
anethum: dill; sweet fennel
anetus: intermittent fever
angina: a sharp, constricting pain; a sore throat; the quinsy (i.e., tonsillitis)

angina maligna: a severe sore throat
angina parotydea: the mumps
angina pectoris: sharp pain in the chest (i.e., muscle spasms)
angina tonsillaris: tonsillitis
angina trachealis: croup
anguis: snake (see also, **serpens**)
angustifolius: narrow-leaved
angustus: narrow
animal: (n.) animal
animalculum (pl. **animalcula**) [a little animal]: a microscopic organism
animalis: (adj.) animal
animo aeger: heartsick physically
animus: life; breath; the mind; the life principle
anisum: anise (see also, **illicium**)
anno interjecto or **anno interiecto**: after the interval of a year
anno vertente: in the course of the year
annos vixit (a.v.): he or she lived (so many years)
annuus: annually; yearly
anodyna: pain-relieving medicines
anserinus: of a goose
antacidus: antacid
ante: before
ante cenam (ant. cen.) or **ante coenam (ant. coen.)**: before supper
ante cibos (a.c. or **ant. cib.)**: before meals
ante cibum (a.c. or **ant. cib.)**: before food
ante dispensationem agita (a.d.a. or **ant. disp. agit.)**: shake before dispensing
ante jentaculum (a.j. or **ant. jentac.)**: before breakfast
ante lucem: before daybreak
ante meridiem or **ante meridianus (a.m.** or **A.M.)**: before noon
ante mortem (a.m. or **A.M.)**: before death
ante partum or **antepartum** [before birth]: before childbirth
ante prandium (ant. prand.): before dinner
antea: beforehand
antebrachium (pl. **antebrachia**): the forearm
anterior: at the front; the front part
anthelmintica: vermifuges; worm remedies
anthelminticus: vermifuge; wormicidal
anti: against; opposed to
anthemis: chamomile

anticardium: the pit of the stomach
anticatarrhalis: an anticatarrhic
anticoagulans: anticoagulant
antidiphthericus: antidiphtherial or antidiphtheriac
antidotum: antidote
antidysentericus: antidysenteric
antidyspepticus: antidyspeptic
antimonialis: antimonial
antimonii vinum: wine of antimony (see also, **vinum antimonii**)
antimonium: antimony (see also, **stibium**)
antineuraligicus: antineuralgic
antisepticus: antiseptic
antitetanicus: antitetanic
antitoxinum: antitoxin
aperiens (aper.): opening; aperient (e.g., a laxative)
apertus: opened; uncovered
apex: the top; the pointed end of the heart (as opposed to **basis cordis**)
aphtha (pl. **aphthae**): an ulcer in the mouth (as in thrush)
apis: a bee
apis mellifica: the honey bee
apium: celery
apo: from; away from
apocynum: dogbane; Canadian hemp
apotheca [a storeroom]: a drugstore
apothecarius [a shopkeeper]: an apothecary
apparatus: an apparatus; equipment; also preparation or provision
applica: apply
applicetur (applicet.): let it be applied
applicentur hirudines vertici: let leeches be applied to the top of the head
apricus: exposed to the sun
aqua (aq.): water
aqua aerata (aq. aerat.): carbonated water
aqua astricta (aq. astr.): frozen water (i.e., ice)
aqua bulliens (aq. bull.): boiling water
aqua caelestis [celestial water]: pure rainwater; also, a cordial
aqua calcis: lime water
aqua calida (aq. calid.): warm water
aqua camphorae: camphor water
aqua Coloniensis: eau de Cologne (see also, **spiritus Coloniensis**)
aqua communis (aq. comm.): common water (i.e., tap water)

aqua destillata (**aq. dest.**): distilled water
aqua dulcis (**aq. dul.**) [sweet water]: fresh water
aqua ex puteo: well water (i.e., water drawn from a well)
aqua fervens (**aq. ferv.**): hot water
aqua fluvialis (**aq. fluv.**): river water
aqua fontana or **aqua fontalis** (**aq. font.**): spring water
aqua fontis (**aq. font.**): spring water
aqua fortis (**aq. fort.**): nitric acid
aqua gelida (**aq. gel.**): cold water
aqua intercus: dropsy (see also, **hydrops**)
aqua marina (**aq. mar.**): seawater
aqua menthae viridis: spearmint water
aqua mirabilis [wonderful water]: an aromatic cordial
aqua naphae (**aq. naph.**): orange-flower water
aqua nivalis (**aq. niv.**): snow water
aqua pluvialis or **aqua pluvia** (**aq. pluv.**): rainwater
aqua pura (**aq. pur.**) [pure water]: distilled water
aqua regia (**aq. reg.**) [royal water]: a mixture of nitric and hydrochloric acids that dissolves platinum and gold
aqua rosae (**aq. ros.**): rose water
aqua saliens (**aq. sal.**): a jet of water
aqua salsa (**aq. sals.**): salty water; salt water
aqua vitae (**aq. vit.**) [water of life]: a distilled spirit (e.g., whiskey)
aqualis: pertaining to water
aquaticus: related to water; aquatic
aquosus: watery
arachis: peanut
aranea: spider
araroba: Goa powder
arbor: a tree
arborescens: treelike
arboreus: pertaining to trees
arcanum (pl. **arcana**) [secret]: a medicine whose composition is closely guarded
arctium lappa: burdock; beggar's button
ardor: a flame or the heat from a flame
ardor febrilis: feverish heat
ardor urinae: burning sensation during urination caused by inflammation of the urethra
ardor ventriculi: heartburn

areca: betel nut
arena: sand
arenosa urina: urine with gravel
areola: the colored area that rings the nipple
argentatus: silvered; silvery
argenteus: of silver; silvery
argentum (Ag. or **ag.**): silver
argentum vivum: mercury; quicksilver
argilla: white clay
aridus [arid]: parched; dried; thirsty
aries: a ram
aristolochia: birthwort
armatus [armed]: provided with
armoracia: horseradish
armus: shoulder; shoulder blade
aromaticus (arom.): aromatic
ars: art; practice
arsenicalis: arsenical
arsenosus: arsenous
arsenum or **arsenicum**: arsenic
arteria aspera: the trachea; the windpipe
arteria magna: the aorta (the artery of the body that carries blood from the heart)
arthriticus: arthritic; also, general joint pain of the body
articulorum dolor [joint pain]: a form of gout
articulus: a joint; a knuckle
artificialis: artificial
artuum: the joints
arvensis: from the field or meadow
arvus: arable land; a ploughed or cultivated field
asafoetida: asafetida
asarum: wild ginger
asarum canadense: Canadian snake root
asbestus: asbestos
ascaris vermicularis: the thread worm
ascensus morbi: increase of a disease
asellus: codfish
asepticus: aseptic
asina: a she-ass
asinus: an ass or donkey

aspidium: the shield fern
aspirinum: aspirin
aspis: asp; adder
asplenium: the spleenwort fern
assidue: constantly
astragalus: milk vetch; also another name for the ankle bone (see **talus**)
astringens: astringent
ater (f. **atra**, neu. **atrum**): coal black
atra et alba: black and white
atropurpureus: a dark purple
attinctus: blackened
attonitus [thunderstruck]: stunned; terrified
audio: to hear
augeatur (aug.): let it be increased
aura: a steam or subtle vapor
aura epileptica: the premonitory sensation of epilepsy sufferers, similar to the sensation of cold fluid rising to the brain
aura seminalis: the principle of attraction that drives semen up the fallopian tubes toward the ovum
aura vitalis: the life principle
aurantiacus: orange (color)
aurantium: an orange (see also, **citrus aurantium**)
aurantius: orange (color)
aurantium amarus: bitter orange
aurantium dulcis: sweet orange
aureus: golden
auri (pl. **auribus**; **aur.**): to or for the ear
auri dextro: to the right ear
auri sinistro: to the left ear
auri lamina: gold leaf (see also, **lamina auri**)
aurinarium (aurin.): an ear cone; an ear suppository
auricula (pl. **auriculae**): the external part of the ear; the earlobe
auris (pl. **aures**): the ear
auris dextra (aur. dext.): the right ear
auris laeva (aur. laev.): the left ear
auristillae (auristill.): ear drops
auritus: having long ears
aurum (Au. or **au.)**: gold
aurum foliatum: gold leaf
australis: southern

autumnalis: autumnal
avellana or **avella**: the filbert
avena: oat grain
avenae farina: oatmeal (see also, **farina avenae**)
avenae sativa: oats
avis: bird
axilla: the armpit (see also, **ala**)
axungia: lard
azymus: unleavened

B

bacca or **baca** (pl. **baccae**): berry
baccatus: producing or bearing berries; berrylike
bacchia: pimpled condition of the face that attends heavy alcohol consumption
bacifer: berry-bearing
bacillus (pl. **bacilli**) [a rod]: a bacillus
bacillum: a small staff or wand; a bougie
baculus: a ball- or oblong-shaped lozenge
balanus [an acorn]: the glans penis and glans clitoridis
balneum or **balineum (baln.)**: bath; bathing room
balneum animale (baln. anima.): part of a freshly killed animal applied to a patient's body or limb
balneum arenae (B.A. or **baln. aren.)**: a sand bath
balneum calidum: a warm bath
balneum fervens: a hot bath
balneum frigidum: a cold bath
balneum Mariae [Mary's bath]: a double boiler, originally used in alchemy
balneum maris (B.M. or **baln. mar.)**: a saltwater bath
balneum medicatum (baln. med.): a medicated bath
balneum siccum (baln. sicc.): a bath of dry ashes
balneum tepidum: a tepid bath
balneum vaporis (B.V. or **baln. vap.)**: a vapor or steam bath
balsamodendron myrrha: myrrh (see also, **myrrha**)
balsameus or **balsamicus**: balsamic
balsamum (balsam.): balsam
baptisia: false or wild indigo
barba: beard

barbatus: bearded
barbitalum: barbital
barium (Ba.): barium
basis (pl. **bases**): base; bottom
basis cordis: the base or rounded end of the heart (as opposed to **apex**)
belladonna: deadly nightshade
bene: well; good
bene decessit [he or she died well]: he or she died naturally
benzenum: benzene; coal naphtha
benzinum: petroleum; gasoline
benzosulfinidum: benzosulfinide (i.e., saccharin sweetener)
berberis: barberry
bergamotta: bergamot
beta: beetroot
betula: sweet birch
betulinus: pertaining to birch
bibe (bib.): drink
bibere: to drink
bibliotheca: a library
bibulus: taking up or taking in water or moisture
bicarbonas: bicarbonate
bicoloratus: having two colors
bicornis: having two horns
biduum: a period or space of two days
biennium: a period or space of two years
bifariam: in two parts
bifurcus: having two forks or prongs
bihorium: two hours
bilibra: two pounds weight
bilis: bile
bini: two each; two at a time; two by two
bipartito: in two parts
bipartitus: divided in two
bipennis: having two wings; also, double-edged
bis: twice
bis bina [twice two]: two pairs
bis in die (b.i.d.): twice a day
bis terve die (b.t.d.): two or three times a day
bis terve in die (b.t.i.d.): two or three times a day

bismuthum (**bisemutum**): bismuth
bitumen: pitch; asphalt
blandus: pleasant; smooth; agreeable
boletus: mushroom
bolus (**bol.**): a large pill
bombacium: cotton (see also, **gossypium**)
bombus: buzzing sound in the ears; gurgling sound in the intestines
bombyx: cotton wadding
bonus: good
boras: borate
borax: sodium borate
borealis: northern
boricus: boric
bos (or **bovis**): an ox
bougium: a bougie (a flexible instrument used for entering the urethra, rectum, *etc.*)
boulimia: unusual or extreme hunger following a meal
bracchium or **brachium**: the arm
brachio (**brach.**): the upper arm; to the arm
branchia: the gill of a fish
brassica: cabbage; broadly, other such vegetables as the turnip and mustard plant
brevicaudatus: short-tailed
brevifolius: having short leaves
brevis: brief; short
breviter: briefly; shortly
brodium: broth; any liquid in which something is boiled
bromidum (**brom.**): bromide
brutus: dull; heavy; without reason
brygmus: grinding of the teeth
bucca: cheek
buffera: buffered
buginarium (**buginar.**): a nasal bougie (i.e., a flexible instrument used for entering the nasal passage)
bulbus: a plant bulb
bulla: blister caused by a burn or by scalding
bulliat (**bull.**): let it boil
bulliens: boiling
bursa [purse]: sac
butyrum (**but.**): butter

butyrum cacaonis: cocoa butter
buxus: box tree; boxwood

C

caballus: a horse
cacao: cocoa seed
cacumen: tip
cadaver: a corpse
caducus: deciduous; perishable
caecitas: blindness
caecus: blind
caeruleus (**caerul.**): blue
caesicius: a bluish-grey
caesios oculos: dim blue or bluish-grey eyes
caesius: blue-grey
cafea or **caffea**: coffee
caffeina: caffeine
cajuputi: cajuput or cajeput; commonly, tea tree
calamina: calamine
calamus: calamus; sweet flag
calcaneum: heel
calcar: spur
calculus (pl. **calculi**): stone or gravel, found chiefly in the kidneys, bladder, and gall ducts
caldaria: a cauldron
calefacere: to warm
calefaciens: warming
calefactus (**cal.**): warmed
calendula: marigold
calide: while warm
calidus: warm; hot
caligo [fog or darkness]: impaired vision; dimness or blindness of vision; also, mental darkness
caligo lentis [defect of the lens]: poor vision; dim vision; a cataract
caligo pupillae: defect of the pupil
caligo retinae: defect of the retina
callum or **callus**: hard; hard skin
callosus: hard-skinned
calomelas (**calom.**): calomel (i.e., subchloride of mercury)

calor: heat; warmth
calva: a bald scalp
calvaria: the human skull
calvus: bald
calx: the heel
calx: lime; limestone; chalk
calx viva: quicklime
cambogia: gamboge (a cathartic)
camelinus: of a camel
camera: a room or chamber
camphora: camphor
camphoratus: camphorated
camphoricus: camphoric
cancer [crab]: the disease cancer
cancrum oris: ulcer of the gums and cheek (i.e., a canker sore); also, cancer of the mouth
candidus: white; clear
canities: grey or greying hair; old age
caninus: canine
canis: dog
canius spasmus: hydrophobic spasms (i.e., spasms caused by rabies)
cannabinus: made of hemp; pertaining to cannabis
cannabis indica: Indian hemp (i.e., a type of hemp from which the narcotic hashish is derived; also known as gunjah or ganja)
cannabis sativa: cannabis; hemp
cannula: a hollow surgical instrument through which fluid is extracted from a tumor or cavity
cantharis: cantharides (i.e., Spanish fly or blister beetle)
caoutchouc: India rubber
capacitas: capacity
cape (cap.): take
capiant (cap.): let them take
capiat (cap.): let him or her take
capiat aeger (f. **aegra**): let the patient take
capiatur (pl. **capianstur**; **cap.**): let it be taken
capiendus (capiend.): to be taken
capillaris: pertaining to the hair; hairlike
capillatus: hairy
capilliculus: the minute veins of the organs
capillus: hair; head of hair

capio: to take
capiti (cap.): to the head
capitiluvium: a head bath; a wash for the head
capsicum: red pepper; cayenne pepper
capsula (cap. or **caps.)** [a small chest]: capsule
capsula amylacea (caps. amylac.): a cachet; a konseal wafer
capsula gelatina (caps. gelat.): a gelatin capsule
capsula vitrea (caps. vitrea): a glass capsule
captus: seized
caput (pl. **capita**): head
caramel or **caramellis**: caramel
carbasus (carbas.): gauze
carbo: carbon; charcoal
carbo animalis: animal charcoal (i.e., bone-black)
carbo ligni: wood charcoal
carbo vegetalilis: in homeopathy, wood charcoal
carbolatus: carbolated
carbolicus: carbolic
carbonarius: a charcoal burner
carbonas: carbonate
carboneum: carbon
cardamomum: cardamom
cardiacus: one suffering heartburn or other stomach pain
cardiopalmus or **cardiotromus**: palpitation of the heart
carica: fig; a dried fig
caricus: of a fig
caries: rottenness; bone or tooth decay
carnarium: a pantry or larder
caro or **carnis**: meat; flesh
carptim [in pieces]: in single portions
carptus: plucked
carpus: the wrist; the bones of the wrist
cartilago: cartilage; gristle
carum: caraway
caruncula [a small piece of flesh]: a carbuncle
caryophyllus: clove (the bud of the **caryophyllus aromaticus**)
cascara sagrada: rhamnus or frangula purshiana; buckthorn
castenea: chestnut
cataplasma (cat. or **catap.** or **cataplasm.)**: a poultice
cataplasma sinapsis: a mustard plaster

cataria: catnip
catharticum or **catharticus**: cathartic; purgative
cathartocarpus: a purgative
catinum or **catinus**: vessel; dish
cauda: the tail of an animal
caulis: stem
causa: cause; reason
causa mortis: because of death (i.e., an awareness that death is approaching)
causticus: caustic
caute: carefully; cautiously
cautus: careful
caveat [let the person beware]: a warning or caution
cavus: hollow; concave
cedrus: cedar tree; juniper
celeriter: quickly
cella: a storeroom
cenatus: after dinner
centifolius: hundred-leaved
centesimus: one-hundredth
centigramma: a centigram
centimetrum: a centimeter
centrum: center; middle point
centrum commune: the solar plexus
centum (cent.): one hundred
cepa: onion; onion plant (see also, **allium cepa**)
cephalagia: a headache
cera: wax
cera alba: white wax (i.e., beeswax bleached by exposure to sunlight)
cera flava: yellow wax (i.e., unbleached beeswax)
ceralis: waxed
cerasus: cherry tree
ceratum (cerat.): cerate (i.e., to wax)
ceratus: waxed
cerealis: cereal
cerebellum: the smaller portion of the brain
cerebrum: the brain
cereolum: a wax bougie
cereolus (cereol.): an urethral bougie
cereus: waxy; waxen

cerevisia: beer
cerifera myrica: bayberry (wax myrtle)
ceriferus: wax-bearing
ceroma [wrestler's ointment]: a fatty tumor of the brain
cerumen: ear wax
cerussa: white lead, used to whiten the face
cerussatus: colored with white lead; painted white
cervix: the back of the neck; a necklike part
cetaceum: spermaceti, a substance obtained from the sperm whale
ceterus: the other part
cetraria: Iceland moss
chalybeatus: pertaining to iron
chamomilla: earth apple, chamomile
charta (**chart.**): paper; powder [wrapped in paper]
charta bibula: blotting paper
charta cerata (**chart. cerat.**): waxed paper
charta exploratoria: test paper
charta exploratoria caerulea: blue litmus paper
chartula (**chartul.**): small paper; small powder [wrapped in paper]
chemia: chemistry
chemicus: chemist
chernibium: a urinal
chininum: quinine
chionanthus [snow flower]: chionanthus or fringe tree
chirurgia: surgery
chirurgicalis or **chirurgicus**: surgical
chirurgus: a surgeon
chloratus or **chlorinatus**: chlorinated
chloroformum: chloroform
chlorum (**cl.**): chlorine
chocolata: chocolate
cholera infantus: infantile cholera
cholera morbus: a non-infectious form of cholera (e.g., gastroenteritis)
cholera nostras: a non-infectious form of cholera
cholericus: bilious; related to cholera
chololithus: biliary calculi (i.e., a gallstone)
chondrus crispus: Irish moss
chorda: cord; gut; suture
chordapsus: spasmatic intestinal colic
chordatus: having a spine

chorea scriptorum: writer's cramp
chromas: chromate
chrysarobinum: chrysarobin (i.e., used as a treatment for skin afflictions)
chrysolithos: topaz
cibus (cib.): food; a meal
cicatricula: a small scar
cicatrix: the scar of a healed cut or sore
cicatrix manet: the scar remains
cicuta maculata: water hemlock (used as a non-medicinal narcotic)
cicuta virosa: poisonous water hemlock
cilia: eyelashes
ciliaris: pertaining to the eyelids or eyelashes
cilium: eyelid; eyelash
cimex: the common bedbug (properly, **cimex lectularius**)
cincinnatus: having curly hair
cincinnus [curled hair]: a lock of hair
cinereus: grey; ashen
cinnamomum: cinnamon
circa (c. or **ca.)**: about; near; around
circinatus: rounded
circiter (**c.** or **circ.**): about
circulus: a circle or ring
circum (**c.** or **circ.**): around; about
circus: circle
cito: swiftly; quickly
cito dispensatur (cito disp.): let it be dispensed quickly
citras: citrate
citreus: pertaining to citrus
citricus: citric
citrullus: watermelon (see also, **cucurbita citrullus**)
citrus: citron tree
citrus aurantium: an orange (see also, **aurantium**)
citrus limetta (or **limetta**): sweet limetta, from which bergamot oil is extracted
citrus limonium (or **limon**): lemon
citrus medica: citron
clathratus: grated; latticed
claudico: to limp
clauditas: lameness
clausus: closed; covered

clava: club
clava herculis [club of Hercules]: pepperwood; prickly ash
clavatus: prickled; having prickles
cnicus benedictus: blessed thistle
coagulare: to coagulate; to curdle
cocae folia: coca leaves
cocaina: cocaine
coccineus: scarlet
coccinus: dyed scarlet
cocculus: a small berry
coccus: an oak berry once thought to be the source of scarlet dye
coccus: cochineal
cochlea or **coclea**: a snail
cochleare (**coch.**) or **cocleare**: spoon; a spoonful
cochleare amplum (**coch. amp.** or **coch. ampl.**): a dessertspoonful
cochleare infantis (**coch. infant.**): a teaspoonful
cochleare magnum (**coch. mag.**): a tablespoonful
cochleare magnum mensura (**coch. mag. mens.**): a measured tablespoonful
cochleare maximum (**coch. max.**): a tablespoonful
cochleare mediocre (**coch. medio.**): a dessertspoonful
cochleare medium (**coch. med.**): a dessertspoonful
cochleare minimum (**coch. min.**): a teaspoonful
cochleare modicum (**coch. mod.**): a dessertspoonful
cochleare parvum (**coch. parv.**): a teaspoonful
cochleare plenum (**coch. plen.**): a tablespoonful
cochlearia magna duo (**coch. mag. ij**): two tablespoonfuls
cochlearia officinalis: scurvy grass
cochlearia parva tria (**coch. parv. iij**): three teaspoonfuls
cochleatim: by spoonfuls; a spoonful at a time
coctilis: baked; cooked
coctio (**coct.**): boiling
coctus: cooked; boiled
codeina: codeine
codex [book]: a formulary
coffea arabica: coffee
cogantur: let them be combined
coitus or **coetus**: sexual union; intercourse
coitus interruptus [interrupted intercourse]: a method of natural birth control

cola (**col.**): strain
cola: kola nut
cola trans chartam: filter or strain through paper
colaturae (**colatur.**): a strained liquid; the substance thus strained
colatus (**colat.**): strained
coleatur (**colet.**): let it be strained
colentur (**colen.**): let them be strained
colica biliosa: colic from an excess of bile in the intestines
colica calculosa: colic from calculi in the intestines
colica meconialis: colic from unexpelled meconium
colica pictorum [painter's colic]: colic from lead in the intestines
collaris: pertaining to the neck; collared
colliculus seminalis: the crest of the urethra
collodium (**collod.**): a collodion
colloidalis: colloidal
collum or **collus**: the neck
collunarium (**collun.**): a nasal douche
collutorium (**collut.**): a mouthwash
collyrium (**coll.** or **collyr.**): an eyewash
colocynthis: bitter apple; bitter cucumber
color: color; tint; complexion
coloratus: colored
coloretur: let it be colored
colum: a sieve; a strainer
columba or **columbus**: pigeon; dove
columna nasi: the dividing wall of the nose
columna oris: the uvula
columna vertebralis: the spinal column
coma: the hair of the head
comans or **comatus**: hairy
comminuere: to diminish; to reduce
comminutus: broken in pieces; crushed
commisce: mix together
commissura: a seam; a joining together
commode: suitably; appropriately; rightly
commodus: suitable; appropriate; satisfactory
communicans [having in common]: diseases that are communicable
communis: common
compos mentis [sound of mind]: in one's right mind
compositus (**comp.**): compound

compressus: compressed; pressed together
conarium: the pineal gland
concentratus: concentrated
concha [seashell]: the hollow portion of the external ear
conchae narium: the spongy bones of the nose
conchus: the orbit of the eyes; the eye cavity
concisus: cut up
concusso prius vitro: the bottle having been previously shaken
concussus: shaken
condimentum (pl. **condimenta**): seasoning; spices taken with food to promote digestion
condire: to pickle
conditus: stored; pickled; seasoned; savory
confectio or **confectum** (**conf.**): a confection
congelatus: frozen; congealed
congius (**C** or **cong.**): a gallon
congressus: coitus
coniferus: cone-bearing
conium: hemlock
conium maculatum: a type of hemlock, given in small doses as a sedative
conjunx or **coniunx** (**con.** or **conj.**): wife; spouse
conjugata diagonalis: diameter of pelvic opening
connubium: marriage; intermarriage
consensus [agreement]: the sympathetic relation between certain organs of the body
conserva (**cons.**): a conserve; a preserve (i.e., a jam or confection)
conserva: keep
consolidus: bound together
consperge (**consperg.**): sprinkle; dust
conspersus: sprinkled
constrictor ani: muscles that close the anus (see also, **sphincter ani**)
constrictor oris: the mouth or lip muscle (also, **orbicularis oris**)
constringentia: astringent
contactus: contact
contagio: contagion (i.e., spreading of a disease through contact)
continuantur remedia (**cont. rem.**): let the remedy be continued
continuetur (**contin.**): let it be continued
contra (**con.**): against
contra bonos mores (**cont. bon. mor.**): contrary to good manners (or morals)

contusus (**cont.**): crushed; bruised
conus: cone
convallaria: lily of the valley
convexus: convex; arched
convivium: a feast or banquet
convolutus: rolled up
convolvulus: bindweed
copia: plenty
coptis: goldthread; canker root
coquatur (**coq.**): let it be boiled
coque (**coq.**): boil
coque ad medietatis consumptionem (**coq. ad med. consump.**): boil to the consumption of half (i.e., render by one-half)
coque in sufficiente quantitate aquae (**coq. in S.Q.A.**): boil in a sufficient quantity of water
coque secundum artem (**coq. S.A.**): boil according to practice (i.e., approved pharmaceutical method)
coquere: to boil
cor: heart
corax: a raven
cordatus: heart-shaped
cordiale: a cordial
cordifolius: having heart-shaped leaves
coriaceus: leathery
coriandrum: coriander
coriandrum satirum: cilantro; also, Chinese parsley
corium: skin; hide; a leather thong
cormus: corm (e.g., a crocus)
corneus: horny; hornlike
cornipes: horn-footed; a hoofed animal
cornix: the crow (see also, **corvus**)
cornu: horn; a horny kind of wart
cornu cervi (**c.c.**): hartshorn
cornu cervi ustum (**c.c.u.**): burnt hartshorn
cornus: dogwood
cornutus: horned
corona veneris: syphilitic blotches around the forehead
coronatus: crowned; encircled
corpori (**corp.**): to the body
corpus (pl. **corpora**): the body

corpus humanum: the human body
corrigens: a corrective (i.e., that part of a prescription meant to modify other ingredients)
corrosivus: corrosive
cortex (cort.): a peel; rind; outer layer (e.g., bark)
cortex limonis: lemon peel
corticatus: having a bark or an outer layer
corvus: the crow (see also, **cornix**)
corylus avellana: hazelnut
corylus maxima: filbert nut
costa: a rib
costatus: ribbed
cotidianus or **cotidie (cotid.)**: daily
coxa: hip; hip joint
cranium: the section of the skull containing the brain
cras: tomorrow
cras mane (c.m.): tomorrow morning (i.e., the next morning)
cras mane sumendus (c.m.s.): to be taken tomorrow morning (i.e., the next morning)
cras nocte (c.n.): tomorrow night
cras nocte sumendus (c.n.s.): to be taken tomorrow night (i.e., the next evening)
cras vespere (c.v.): tomorrow evening
crassamentum: a clot of blood
crassus: thick; dense; solid
crastinus (crast.): of tomorrow; on the morrow
cremor: cream
crenulatus: notched; scalloped
creosotum: creosote
crepitus (crep.): discharge of wind or gas from the bowels
crepusculum (crepus.): twilight; in the evening
creta: chalk
creta praeparata: prepared or washed chalk
cribratus: sifted
cribrum: a sieve
cribrum ferreum: a wire sieve
cribrum setaceum: a hair sieve
crinis: hair
crispus: curled
cristatus: having a crest (see also, **iubatus** or **jubatus**)

croceus or **crocinus**: saffron yellow; golden yellow
crocus: the crocus; saffron (properly, **crocus sativus**)
crudus: crude
cruentus: blood-stained; blood-soaked
cruri: to the leg
crus (pl. **crura**): a leg or shank; the shinbone
crustulum: a tart or pastry
crux medicorum: the crux or puzzle of doctors
crystallinus: crystalline
crystallizatus: crystallized
crystallus: crystal
cubeba: cubeb pepper
cubiculum: a bedroom
cubicus: cubic
cubitalis: of the elbow; a cubit in length
cubitum: the elbow; the forearm
cubitus: a lying down
cucumis: a cucumber
cucurbatio: cupping
cucurbita [gourd]: a cupping-glass
cucurbita citrullus: watermelon (see also, **citrullus**)
cucurbita pepo: pumpkin (see also, **pepo**)
cucurbita sicca: a glass used for dry cupping
cui: which; to or for whom
cujus: of which
cujus libet (**cuj. lib.**): of whatever pleases
cultellus: knife
cum (**c̄**): with
cum aqua (**c̄ aq.**): with water
cum cibos (**c̄ c.**): with meals
cum cibum (**c̄ c.**): with food
cum creta: with chalk
cum duplo (**c̄ dup.**): with twice as much
cum parte aequale (**c̄ pt. aeq.**): with an equal quantity
cum penicillo (**c̄ pen.**): with a camel-hair brush
cum semisse (**c̄ sem.**): with an added half
cum tanto (**c̄ tant.**): with as much
cummiphorus (**commiphorus**): gum-bearing (see also, **gummifer**)
cuneifolius: having wedge-shaped leaves
cuneus: wedge

cuprum (cu.): copper
cura: care; healing
curatio (curat.) [healing]: the treatment of disease; also, a dressing
curatus: cared for
curcuma: turmeric
cuspidatus: a pointed tooth
cutis: the skin
cutis anserina [goose flesh]: goose bumps or goose pimples
cutis capitis: the scalp
cyanidum: cyanide
cyatho theae: in a cup of tea
cyathus [a ladle used for filling wine glasses]: a wine glass; a wineglassful
cyathus amplus (cyath. amp.): a tumblerful
cyathus magnus (cyath. mag.): a tumblerful
cyathus medius (cyath. med.): a small tumbler or claret glassful
cyathus modicus (cyath. mod.): a small tumbler or claret glassful
cyathus parvus (cyath. parv.): a wineglassful
cyathus vinarius (cyath. vinar.): a wineglassful
cyathus vinosis (cyath. vin.): a wineglassful
cydonium: the quince fruit; quince seed

D

da (d.): give
dandus (dand.): to be given
dare: to give
datura: thorn apple
de: of; concerning; from
de die: while still day
de die in diem (de d. in d.): from day to day
de nocte: while still night
deaurare: to gild; to coat
deaurentur pilulae (deaur. pil.): let the pills be gilded (i.e., coated)
debilitas: weakness
debita spissitudine (deb. spiss.): of a proper thickness or consistency
decandrus: having ten stems
decanta (dec.): pour off
decem: ten
deceptio visus: an optical illusion

decigramma (**dg.** or **dgrm.**): a decigram
decimillilitra (**decimil.**): a decimilliliter
decimus: the tenth
decoctio or **decoctum** (**decoct.**): a decoction
decoctum hordei: barley water
decoctus: boiled; boiled down
decoloratus: decolorized
decoquere: to boil down
decorticatus: peeled (i.e., the bark having been removed)
decubitus (**decub.**): lying down; having gone to bed
decubitus hora (**decub. hor.**): at bedtime
defaecatus: cleaned; refined
defectio or **defectio animi**: fainting; a fainting spell
defectum animae: fainting; a fainting spell
deflagratus: consumed by fire
deformitas: deformity
deformis: deformed
deglutiat: let him or her swallow
deglutiatur (**deglut.**): let it be swallowed
deglutio: to swallow
dehydratus: dehydrated
deicio: to throw up
deinde (or **dein**): then; next; finally
dejectiones alvi (**dej. alv.**): evacuation of the bowels (i.e., stools)
delenimentum: anything that soothes
delibutus: steeped
delicatus: soft; tender
delinquescens: deliquescent
deliquium: falling or fainting
delirium tremens (**D.T.**) [trembling delirium]: mental delusions caused by alcohol poisoning
delphinium: larkspur seed
demens: out of one's mind; insane
dementia: insanity
dementia a potu [insanity from drinking]: delirium tremens
dementia praecox: a form of early insanity
demortuus: the late (i.e., deceased)
demulcens: softening; soothing
demum: at length
denigratus: blackened

denigrescens: non-staining; stainless
denique: at last; finally
dens (pl. **dentis**): a tooth
dens canis: a dog tooth
dens expolitor: a tooth polish
dens leonis: a lion tooth
dentatus: having teeth; toothed
dentes cuspidati [the pointed teeth]: the canines; the eye teeth
dentes incisores [the biting teeth]: the incisors
dentes molares [the grinding teeth]: the molars
dentes sapientia: the wisdom teeth
dentifricium: dentifrice; tooth powder
dentilinimentum: dental liniment
dentium cortex: the enamel coating of the teeth
dentur (**d.**): let them be given
dentur tales doses iv (**d.t.d. iv**): let four such doses be given
deodoratus: deodorized
depilatorium (**depilat.**): a depilatory
depurantia: medicines used to purify the blood
depuratus: purified
derma: skin
dermatologicus: dermatological
derosus: gnawed away
desperandum: to be hopeless
despumatus: skimmed; clarified
destillatus: distilled
desudatio: sweating
detannatus: tannin-free
detergens: detergent; cleansing
detoxicatus: non-toxic
detritus [a rubbing away]: waste matter from washing or erosion
detur (**d.**): let it be given
detur talis dosis (**d.t.d.** or **D.T.D.**): give of such a dose
dexter: right
dextra or **dextera**: the right hand
dextrosum: dextrose
diaeta: diet; a daily regimen
diagnosticus: diagnostic
dialysatus: dialyzed
diarrhoea: diarrhea

dictus [said]: prescribed; indicated
diebus alternis (**dieb. alt.**): every other day
diebus tertiis (**dieb. tert.**): every third day
diem ex die (**d. ex d.**): from day to day
dies: day or daytime
dies natalis: birthday
diffusus: diffused
digestivus: digestive
digitalis: digitalis; foxglove
digitatus: having fingers and toes
digitus: finger; toe; a finger's breadth (i.e., one inch)
digitus anularius: the ring finger
digitus auricularis: the little finger
digitus index: the index finger
digitus medius: the middle finger
digitus pedis: a toe
digitus pollex: the thumb or big toe
dilapsus: effloresced
dilatationem: a widening; a dilation
dilatio: delaying; a postponement or delay; an interval
dilubilis: dilutable
diluculo: at daybreak
diluculum (**diluc.**): the break of day; in the morning
dilue (**dil.**): dilute or dissolve
dilutus or **dilutum** (**dil.** or **dilut.**): diluted; faint
dimidium (**dimid.**): half; the half
dimidius (**dim.**): one-half
dioicus: unisexual
dioscorea: wild yam
dioxidum: dioxide
diphthericus: diphtheria
directio: a direction; the act of directing
directione propria (**d.p.** or **D.P.** or **direc. prop.**): with proper directions
dispensa (**disp.**): dispense
dispensatorium: a handbook on the preparation and use of various medicines
dispensatus: distributed by weight
distalis: distal; the farther end
distoma hepaticum: distoma (the fluke-worm; see also, **fasciola hepatica**)

disulfidum or **disulphidum**: disulfide or disulphide
diureticus: diuretic
diurnus: lasting for a day; day-long
diutinus or **diuturnus**: long-lasting; continuing long
diverticulum: a sac
dives (favored by the gods): rich; a rich person
dividatur (**div.**): let it be divided
dividatur in partes aequales (**d. in p. aeq.** or **div. in par. aeq.**): let it be divided into equal parts
divide (**div.**): divide
dolens: painful
dolenti parti (**dolent. part.**): to the painful part
dolentibus partibus (**dolent. part.**): to the painful parts
dolor: pain
dolor artuum: gout
dolor capitis: pain of the head
dolor dentium: pain of the teeth
dolor faciei: pain of the face
dolore urgente (**dol. urg.**): with the onset of pain; when the pain is severe
dolores corporis: bodily ills
domesticus: domestic
domi [in the house]: at home
domus: home
donec (**don.**): until
donec alvus soluta fuerit: until the bowels are loosened
donec dolor leniat: until the pain lessens
donec dolor leniatur: until the pain is relieved
donec dolor exulaverit: until the pain is relieved
donec doloris mitigatio sit: until the pain eases
donec evomuerit: until the patient may have vomited
donec liquescat: until it melts
donec perfecte coeant: until they mix perfectly
donec sedatur vomitio: until vomiting is allayed
donec somnus obrepat: until sleep comes on
donum: a gift
dorsum: the back
dosi pedetentim crescente: by gradually increasing the dose
dosibus dividuis: in divided doses
dosibus exiquis: in small doses

dosibus magnis: in large doses
dosibus repetitis: in repeated doses
dosis (dos.): dose
dosis augeatur ad guttas ij (dos. aug. ad gtt. ij): let the dose be increased to two drops
dosis augeatur ad guttas iij (dos. aug. ad gtt. iij): let the dose be increased to three drops
dosis augeatur ad guttas iv (dos. aug. ad gtt. iv): let the dose be increased to four drops
drachma (dr. or **dram.)**: a drachm (i.e., one-eighth of an ounce)
dryopteris: wood fern; oak fern; buckler fern
dubius: doubtful
ducenti: two hundred
ductilis: plastic (i.e., able to be shaped)
ductus: duct; canal
ductus aquosi: the lymphatic ducts
ductus ejaculatorius: the duct that carries the semen into the urethra
dulcedo: sweetness; agreeableness
dulcis: sweet
dulcis unda: fresh water
dum: while
dum febris absit: while fever is absent
dum febris adsit: while fever is present
duo: two
duo cum semisse: two and a half
duo sextarii: a quart
duodecim: a dozen
duodeviginti: eighteen
duplex: double; twofold
duplum (dup.): twice as much
duplus: double the amount
dura mater: the external membrane of the brain
durans: during, lasting, enduring
durante: during; continuing
durante dolore (dur. dolor.): during the pain; the pain continuing
durante febre (dur. feb.): during the fever (see also, **febre durante**)
duratus: hardened; dried
durus: rough; hard
dysentericus: dysentery

E

e lacte (**e lact.**): with milk
e paullo or **e paulo**: in a little; with a little
e paullo aquae (**e paul. aq.**): with a little water
e pauxillo aquae (**e paux. aq.**): with very little water
e quolibet vehiculo (**e quol. veh.**): with any vehicle
e quovis liquido (**e quov. liq.**): with any liquid
e vehiculo crasso (**e vehic. crass.**): in a thick vehicle
e vino (**e vin.**): with wine
eadem (**ead.**): the same
ebriolus: mildly intoxicated
ebrius: drunk; intoxicated
ebur: ivory
eburneus (**eburn.**): made of ivory
ecballium: squirting cucumber
echinatus: spiny
echinus: a hedgehog; also, a sea urchin
eclampsia: a violent onset; a sudden development or complication
edens: eating
edentatus: lacking teeth; toothless
edulcora (**ed.**): sweeten; to make more palatable
edulcoratus (**ed.**): sweetened; made palatable; also, clarified
edulis: edible
effeminatus: effeminate
effervescens: effervescent
effervescentia: effervescence
efficaciter: effectively
efficiens: being efficient; effective
effluvium: vaporous stench from decaying matter
effunde: pour out
ejusdem (**ejusd.**): of the same
egestus (pl. **egesta**): waste matter
ego: I
elaeosaccharum or **eleosaccharum**: oil sugar (see also, **oleosaccharum**)
elapsus: elapsed
elastica: rubber; India rubber
elasticus: elastic
eleatior: taller
electuarium (**elect.**): an electuary (i.e., a confection)

electus: elected; chosen
elettaria: cardamom
elixir (elix.) [a magical potion]: a medicinal liquid, such as cough medicine
embrocatio: an embrocation; a rubbing oil or liniment
emeticus: emetic
emolliens: softening
empiricus: an unscientific physician; a quack (i.e., a physician who relies on practical rather than scientific knowledge)
emplastrum (emp.; pl. **emplastra**): a plaster or topical application
emplastrum lyttae: a blistering plaster or application
emplastrum vesicatorium: a blistering plaster or application
emulgens: emulsifying
emulsio or **emulsum (emul.** or **emuls**): an emulsion
enema (en. or **enem.**; pl. **enemata**): an enema; a clyster
ens: being
entericus [enteric]: intestinal; pertaining to the intestines
epicranium: the scalp
epidemicus: epidemic
epidipnis: dessert
epigastrium: the upper region of the abdomen below the sternum
epispasticus: blistering
epistomium (epistom.): a stopper; a bung or plug
epistomium suberinum: a cork stopper
epistomium vitreum: a glass stopper
epithelium: cuticular areas of the body that differ from normal skin, such as the lips and nipples
epitonium [a turncock or bung]: a genus of sea snail
eques: an equestrian
equinus: equine
equus: a horse
erectus: upright
ergo: therefore
ergota: ergot (of rye)
erigeron: fleabane
eriodictyon: yerba santa
erosus: eroded; corroded
erythema: a simple skin rash
erythroxylon: coca
escharoticus: caustic; producing a scab or scar
esculentus: edible

essentia: essence
esuriens (**esur.**): fasting
et alia (**et al.**): and other things
et alibi (**et al.**): and elsewhere
et alii or **et aliae** (**et al.**): and others
et cetera (**etc**.): and the rest; and so on
et conjunx (**et conj**): and spouse
et uxor (**et ux.**): and wife
eugenia caryophyllus: clove tree
evacuatio: an evacuation; an emptying
evanescere (**evan.**): to disappear; vanish; weaken
evanesco (**evan.**): to disappear; vanish; weaken
evanuerit: it shall have disappeared
evaporans: evaporating
ex aliquo idoneo vehiculo: in any suitable vehicle
ex aqua (**ex aq.**): in water
ex aqua frigida: in cold water
ex cyatho parvo: in a small cupful
ex modo praescripto (**e.m.p.**): after the manner prescribed
ex morbo convalescere: to recover from a disease
ex parte: partly; in part
ex sanguis [without blood]: deathly pale
ex somnis: sleepless
ex tempore or **extempore**: at or on the moment; at once
ex vulnere mori: to die of wounds
excelsus: tall; high
excessus e vita: departure from life
excipiens: an excipient (i.e., an inert substance added to a prescription medicine)
excrementum (pl. **excrementa**): human excrement
exempli gratia (**e.g.**): for example
exemplum: example
exhibe: give; shown; allow
exhibeatur (**exhib.**): let it be exhibited or given
exhibendus: to be given
exoneratus: relieved
exoticus: foreign; exotic
expectorans: expectorant
expers: without
expolitus: smooth; polished

expressus: pressed out; squeezed out
exprimo: to squeeze out
exsanguis: bloodless
exsiccatus: thoroughly dried
exsucidus: juiceless
extemplo: directly; immediately
extende (**ext.**): spread; apply
extende super alutam (**ext. sup. alut.**): spread upon leather
extensus: extended; spread
externus: external
extractum (**ext.** or **extr.**): an extract

F

faba: bean
fac (**F.** or **f.**): make
facies: the face
facies rubra: redness in the face
facile: easily
facilis: easy
factitius: artificial; manufactured
faeces (**feces**): dung; excrement
faex: sediment; the dregs
fallax: deceptive; fallacious
falx: a sickle
fames: hunger
farfara: coltsfoot (see also, **tussilago**)
farina (**far.**): flour; meal
farina avenae: oatmeal (see also, **avenae farina**)
farinosus: farinaceous; starchy (i.e., foods consisting of or containing starch)
farrago: fodder
farreus: made of corn or meal
fartim (or **fartem**): minced meat stuffing
fascia: a bandage; a binding
fascia spiralis [spiral binding]: a type of bandage that is wound around the limb in spiral fashion
fasciculus: a packet
fasciola: a small bandage
fasciola hepatica: the fluke-worm (also **distoma hepaticum**)

fastigiatus: tapering
fauces: pharynx; the throat
faucibus internis: inside the throat
favus: honeycomb
favus [honeycomb]: crusty yellow pustules of the scalp, symptomatic of ringworm
febre durante (feb. dur.): during the fever; the fever continuing (see also, **durante febre**)
febricula: a slight fever
febriculosus: feverish
febrifugus: having fever relieving or moderating properties
febrilis: feverish
febris (pl. **febres**): a fever
febris carcerum [jail fever]: typhus gravior; typhoid fever
febris castrensis [camp fever]: typhus gravior; typhoid fever
febris quartana or **quartana**: a fever occurring every fourth day, as in malaria
fecula: starch
fel: the gallbladder; bile
fel bovinum: ox gall
fel bovinum purificatum: purified ox bile
felinus: feline
felis: cat
felix: happy
fellifluus: flowing with bile
femina (f.): female; a woman
femoribus: [to] the thighs
femoribus internis: [to] the inner thighs
femur: the thigh
fenestra [window]: an opening
ferax or **fertilis**: fertile; fruitful
fere or **ferme**: almost; nearly; about; (neg.) scarcely
fermentatus: fermented
fermentum: yeast
ferox: fierce; wild
ferratus [ferrated]: containing iron; iron colored
ferreus: made of iron
ferri limaturae: iron filings
ferrosus: ferrous (i.e., containing or consisting of iron)
ferrugineus: rusty; rust-colored; tasting of iron

ferrugo: rust; rust-colored
ferrum (**Fe.** or **ferr.**): iron
fertilis: fertile; fruitful
fertilitas: fertility
ferula: asafetida
ferus: wild
fervens (**ferv.**): hot; boiling
fervente die: in the heat of the day
fervidus: boiling hot
fessus: tired; weary
festinato: hastily
fetus or **foetus**: offspring
fiant (**f.** or **ft.**): let them be made
fiant chartae (**ft. chart.**): let papers (or powders) be made
fiant pilulae (**ft. pil.**): let pills be made
fiant suppositoria (**ft. suppos.**): let suppositories be made
fiant trochisci (**ft. troch.**): let lozenges be made
fiat (**f.** or **ft.**) [let it be so]: let it be made
fiat cataplasma (**ft. cataplasm.**): let a poultice be made
fiat ceratum (**ft. cerat.**): let a cerate be made
fiat collyrium (**ft. collyr.**): let an eyewash be made
fiat confectio (**ft. confec.**): let a confection be made
fiat electuarium (**ft. elect.**): let an electuary be made
fiat emplastrum (**ft. emp.**): let a plaster be made
fiat emulsum (**ft. emuls.**): let an emulsion be made
fiat experimentum in corpore vili: let the experiment be done upon a worthless body (or object)
fiat gargarisma (**ft. garg.**): let a gargle be made
fiat haustus (**ft. haust.**): let a draft be made
fiat infusum (**ft. infus.**): let an infusion be made
fiat injectio (**ft. inject.**): let an injection be made
fiat lege artis (**f.l.a.** or **F.L.A.**): let it be made according to practice or the usual method
fiat linimentum (**ft. linim.**): let a liniment be made
fiat massa (**ft. mas.**): let a lump or a mass be made
fiat mistura (**ft. mist.**): let a mixture be made
fiat pulvis (**ft. pulv.**): let a powder be made
fiat pulvis subtilis (**ft. pulv. subtil.**): let a fine powder be made
fiat secundum artis regulas (**f.s.a.r.** or **F.S.A.R.**): let it be made according to the rules of practice

fiat solutio (**ft. solut.**): let a solution be made
fiat unguentum (**ft. ung.**): let an ointment be made
fiat venaesectio (**ft. venaes.**): let a vein be bled
fibra: fiber
fictile: an earthenware container
fictilis: earthen; of clay
ficus: fig
fides: faith; trust
filia: daughter
filicis maris: male fern
filius: son
filix: a fern
filtra: filter or strain
filtrum: a filter
filum: a thread
fimbria (pl. **fimbriae**) [fringe]: the fringe-like areas on the ends of the fallopian tubes
fimus or **fimum**: filth; dung
finis: the end
fistula: pipe; a small tube; an internal ulcer
fistula armata: a fountain syringe
fistula in ano: an anal ulcer
fixus: fixed
flamma: flame
flatus: flatulence
flavus (**flav.**): yellow
flexibilis or **flexilis**: flexible; pliant; supple
flocci volitantes [flying specks]: a type of vision impairment in which one sees faint objects flying or floating before the eyes (see also, **muscae volitantes** or flying flies)
floccus: a tuft of wool
floridus: flowery; bright
flos: flower
flos unguentorum: the flower of ointments
fluctus: wave; a flowing; an outflow
fluidrachma: a fluid drachm
fluidextractum or **fluidum extractum** (**fldext.** or **fldxt.**): fluidextract
fluiduncia: a fluid ounce
fluidus (**fl.** or **fld.**): fluid; liquid
fluoridum: fluoride

foeniculum: fennel
foetidus: fetid; stinking
folium (fol.): a leaf
fomentum: fomentation
fons or **fontis**: spring; fountain
fontana: a fountain
fontanus: from a spring
foramen: aperture; opening; hole
foramen magnum [great opening]: the passage from the cranial cavity to the spinal canal
foratus: pierced
forceps: a pair of tongs
forfex: a pair of scissors
forma: shape; form
formaldehydum: formaldehyde
formalis: formal; having a set form
formatus: formed
formica: an ant
formosus: beautiful; well-formed
formula (pl. **formulae**) [formula]: a set form; a method; a prescription
fornax: oven; furnace
fortior: stronger
fortior vino: stronger than wine
fortis (fort.): strong
fortissimus: strongest
fossa (pl. **fossae**): ditch; depression; hollow area
fotus: fomentation
fovea (pl. **foveae**): a small pit or depression; a small hollow area
fovea centralis: the center the retina in which vision is the most acute
foveola (pl. **foveolae**): a small pit
fracta dosi (fract. dos.): broken into doses; in divided doses
fractura: fracture; a break in the bone
fractus: broken
fragilis: fragile; brittle
fragilitas ossium: brittleness of the bones
fragrans: fragrant
frangula: buckthorn
frater: brother
fraxinus: the ash tree
fremitus: vibration

frendere: to grind
frendo: to gnash or grind the teeth; grind up small
frequens: frequent; repeated
frequenter (freq.): frequently
frequentissime: very frequently
fricamentus: rubbing
fricare: to rub
fricatur: let it be rubbed
frictio: friction
frigidus or **frigus**: cold; chilly
frigor: the cold
frons: forehead
frontis: front
fructus (fruct.): fruit
frugi: useful; honest; moderate; also, fit to eat
frumentum: corn; grain
frustillatim (frust.) (bit by bit): in small bits; in little pieces
frustum: a morsel
frutescens: bush-like
frutex: a shrub
frux (pl. **fruges**): fruit; fruits of the earth
fucus: bladderwrack; seaweed
fulmine ictus: struck by lightning
fulvus: yellow; tawny; brown
fumans: fuming
fumus: smoke
fundo: to pour out
fundus: bottom; the base of an organ
fungus: fungus; a mushroom
funis: cord; rope
furca: fork
furcatus: forked
fuscus: brown; dark
fusus: fused; molded; melted

G

gadi iecur: cod liver
gadus morrhua or **gadus**: the codfish
galbeus or **galbeum**: a headband or armband; a bandage for the arm

galbinus: greenish-yellow
galea [helmet]: a type of headache; a head bandage
galla: nutgall
gallina: a hen
gallinaceus: pertaining to poultry
gargarisma (**garg.**): a gargle
gas or **gasum** (pl. gasa): gasf
gaster: stomach; belly
gaultheria: wintergreen (properly, **gaultheria procumbens**)
gelasinus: a dimple (on the cheek)
gelatina or **gelatum**: gelatin; jelly
gelatina quavis (**gel. quav.**): in any kind of jelly
gelatina ribesiorum: currant jelly
gelatinum or **gelatum**: gelatin; jelly
gelatinus: of gelatin
gelatus: frozen
gelidus: cold
gelsemium: yellow jasmine
geminus (pl. **gemini**): twin; double
gemma: a bud
gena (pl. **genae**): the cheek
geneticus: pertaining to the procreative function
geniculum: knee joint; kneecap
genticulatus: knotty
genu: knee
genua valga: a deformity that results in knocked knees
genus or **generis**: genus; kind
geratici: a class of diseases
geraticus: old age
germen: sprout; bud; germ
gibbus: hump
gingiva (pl. **gingivae**): gum; the gums
glabbella: the space between the eyebrows
glaber: smooth; hairless; bald
glacialis: icy; pertaining to glaciers
glacies: ice
gladius: swordlike
glandula: gland; a small gland
glandulosus: having kernels
glans: an acorn; a chestnut

glans clitoridis: the glans of the clitoris
glans penis: the glans of the penis
glaucoma: a cataract
glaucus: greenish-grey; bluish-grey
gleba or **glaeba**: a lump or mass
globula: globule
globulus: a small round mass or ball, such as a pill or suppository
glomus: a ball of thread or yarn; a skein
glonoinum [glonoin]: nitrogylcerin
glossa: tongue
glucosum: glucose
glusidum: saccharin
gluten [glue]: gluten
gluteus maximus: the major muscle of the buttocks
glutineus or **glutinosus**: sticky
glycerinatus: glycerinated
glyceritum (glyc. or **glycer.** or **glyct.**): glycerite
glycyrrhiza: licorice
gossypium (gossyp.): cotton (see also, **bombacium**)
gossypium absorbens: absorbent cotton (i.e., cotton wool)
gradatim (grad.) [step by step]: gradually or by degrees
gradus: step; degree
gramen: grass
gramineus: grassy
gramma (grm.): a gram
granatum: pomegranate (see also, **punica granatum**)
grandiflorus: large-flowered
graniticus: related to granite; granitelike
granulatus: granulated
granulum: granule
granum (gr. or **grn.**; pl. **grana**): grain
granum cum semisse: one grain and a half
gratis: favor; no cost
gratus (grat.): pleasant; agreeable
graveolens: strong-smelling
gravidus uterus: the condition of the uterus during gestation
gravis: grave; serious; weighty
gregarius: of the flock or herd; sociable
grex: flock; herd; band of people
grindelia: California gum plant

grossus: large; coarse; unrefined
gryllus: cricket; grasshopper
gul attar: attar of roses
gummi: gum
gummi Arabicum: gum Arabic
gummi Armeniacae: apricot gum
gummi gutti gambiae (g.g.g.): gamboge
gummi mimosae: gum acacia
gummifer: gum-bearing (see also, **cummiphorus**)
gummosus: gummy
gurges: a whirlpool or eddy
gustus: taste
gutta (g. or **gt.)**: a drop
gutta rosea [rosy drop]: a premodern term for **acne rosacea (rosacea)**, i.e., acne
guttae (gtt.): drops
guttatim (guttat.): by drops; drop by drop
guttiferus or **guttifera**: gamboge-bearing; gum-bearing
guttis quibusdam (gutt. quibus.): with a few drops
guttur: throat; windpipe
gutturi (gutt.): to or for the throat
gutturi applicandus (gutt. appl.): to be applied to the throat
gymnicus or **gymnasticus**: gymnastic
gyrus: a circle or ring; the spiral cavity of the ear

H

habeat (habt.) (pl. **habent**): let him or her have
hac nocte (hac noct.): tonight; this night
haematoxylon: logwood
haemoptysis: spitting of blood
haemorrhagia: continued bleeding
haesitantia linguae: a speech impediment
halitus: exhalation; breath; vapor arising from newly drawn blood
hallex: the thumb; the big toe
halo: to exhale or breathe out
hama: a bucket or pail; a vessel for holding wine
hamamelis: witch hazel
hamatus: hooked; crooked
hamus: a fish hook; thorn

harum: of these
haud satis: not enough
hauriat: let him or her drink
hauriatur in fauces: let it be drawn into the throat
haustus (**haust.**): a draught; a drink
hebdomada (**hebdom.**): a week; a seven-day period
hebdomas: the seventh day of a disease (said to be a critical day)
hedera: ivy
helenium: sneezeweed
helianthus annuus: the sunflower
helonias: false unicorn
hepar: liver (see also, **jecur**)
hepatarius: related to the liver
hepatolithus: calculus of the liver
herba: herb; grass
herbeus: green like grass
heri: yesterday
herinacius: a porcupine
hermaphroditus: an hermaphrodite
hernia: rupture
hernia humoralis: inflammation of the testicle
hernia inguinalis: hernia of the groin
herpes circinatus: ringworm
herpes zoster: shingles
hesterna nocte: yesterday night; last night
hibernus [of winter]: for the winter
hibiscum: hibiscus; the marsh mallow
hibridus or **hybridus**: hybrid
hic, **haec** or **hoc**: this; in this place
hic sepultus est (**h.s.e.**): here lies buried
hiems: winter
hippoglossus: halibut
hippurus: fish (i.e., a gilt-head or goldfish)
hircismus [goat smell]: armpit odor
hircosus: smelling like a goat
hirsutus (covered with hair): hairy; bristly
hirudo (**hir.** or **hirud.**): a leech
his adde: add to these
hispidus: bristly; shaggy; prickly
histamina: histamine

hodie: today
homicidium [homicide]: murder; manslaughter
homo: man
homo erectus [upright man]: an early species of human which stood upright
homo sapiens [wise man]: the human species of the genus Homo
hoc loco (**h.l.**): in this place
hoc vespere (**hoc vesp.**): this evening
hora (**H.** or **hor.**): hour
hora amplius: over an hour
hora antemeridiana: in the forenoon
hora decubitus (**h.d.** or **H.D.** or **hor. decub.**): at bedtime
hora postmeridiana: in the afternoon
hora somni (**h.s.** or **H.S.**): at bedtime
hora somni sumendus: to be taken at bedtime
hora vespertina: in the evening hour
horae quadrante (**hor. quad.** or **hor. quadrant.**): a quarter of an hour
horae unius spatio (**hor. un. spat.**): after one hour
hordeum: barley
hordeum decorticatum: pearl barley
horis alternis: every other hour
horis intermediis (**hor. interim.**): at intermediate hours
horridus: cold shivers
hortensis: from the garden
hortus: garden
hospes or **hospita** [stranger]: guest; host
hospitum [hospitality]: a guest chamber
humanus: human; pertaining to human beings
humerus or **umerus**: the shoulder; the upper arm
humescens: becoming wet or moist; deliquescent
humi: on the ground
humidus: damp; wet; moist
humor or **umor** [moisture]: any body fluid other than blood (e.g., bile)
humulus: hops (properly, **humulus lupulus**; see also, **lupulus**)
hybridus or **hibridus**: hybrid
hydrargyrum (**hg.** or **hydr.**): mercury; quicksilver
hydrastis: golden seal
hydratus: hydrated
hydrocephalus: dropsy of the brain

hydrochloricus: hydrochloric
hydrogenium: hydrogen
hydrolatum: a distilled water
hydrophobia [fear of water]: inability to swallow liquids
hydropicus: dropsical
hydrops: dropsy (see also, **aqua intercus**)
hydrops siccus [dry dropsy]: tympanites
hydrosus: hydrous; aqueous (i.e., watery)
hydroxidum: hydroxide
hydrus: a water snake
hyoscyamus: henbane
hypericum perforatum: St. John's wort
hypodermicus: hypodermic
hypogastrium: the lower part of the abdomen
hypophysis: the pituitary gland
hyssopus: hyssop

I

ibidem (**ibid.** or **ib.**): in the same place
ictericus: jaundiced
icterus: jaundice
ictus solis: sunstroke
id est (**i.e.**): that is
idcirco: for that reason; for that purpose
idem: the same
idem quod: the same as
identidem: repeatedly
idoneus: appropriate; suitable
iecur or **jecur**: the liver (see also, **hepar**)
ientaculum or **jentaculum** (**ient.** or **ientac.**): breakfast
ignatia: St. Ignatius' bean
ignis: fire
ignis actualis [actual fire]: cautery of the flesh by fire or heated iron
ignis sacer [sacred fire]: erysipelas
ignis sancti Antonii [St. Anthony's fire]: erysipelas
ilium: the hip bone
illicium: star anise (properly, **illicium anisatum**)
illico (**illic.**): immediately
illinendus (**illinend.**): to be smeared

imberbis or **imberbus**: beardless
immanis: huge
immaturus: unripe
immedicatus: unmedicated
implicatus: implicated; entangled; entwined
impluvium: rainwater basin
impolitus: unpolished
impollutus: undefiled
impransus: fasting
imprimis: first; in the first place
impurus: impure
in actu effervescentiae: in a state of or while effervescing
in aquis rapide fluentibus: in rapidly flowing water
in aquis quietis: in still waters
in articulo mortis: at the point or moment of death
in aurem dextram (in aur. dext.): into the right ear
in aurem sinistram (in aur. sinist.): into the left ear
in cauda venenum: in the tail is the venom
in cubiculo: in the bedroom (i.e., while reclining)
in corpore vili: upon a worthless body (or object)
in decocto hordei: in barley water
in dies (in d.) or **indies (ind.)**: from day to day; daily
in dorso: in or on the back
in dubio [in doubt]: undetermined
in extremis: at the point of death
in fauces: in or into the throat
in folio argenti: in silver leaf
in folio auri: in gold leaf
in horas: hourly
in incertum: for an indefinite period
in lacte: in milk
in lacte exhibendus: to be given in milk
in languoribus: in fainting spells
in lecto: in bed
in loco: in place of; in lieu of
in loco frigido: in a cool place
in melius mutari: to take a turn for the better
in oculum dextrum (in ocul. dext.): into the right eye
in oculum sinistrum (in ocul. sinist.): into the left eye
in partes aequales: into equal parts

in phiala: in a bottle
in pulmento (in pulm.): in gruel
in quovis liquido: in any liquid
in quovis vehiculo: in any vehicle
in scatula: in a box
in singulas aures (in sing. aur.): into each ear
in singulo: in each
in statu effervescentiae: in a state of or while effervescing
in summa aqua: on the surface of the water
in tempus [for a time]: temporarily
in toto: in all; completely
in utero (in ut.): in the womb
in vacuo: in a vacuum
in vase aperto: in an uncovered vessel
in vase leviter clauso: in a lightly covered vessel
in vase operto: in a covered vessel
in vicem: alternately; by turns
in vitro (in vit.) [in a glass]: in a test tube or petri dish
in vivo: in the living organism
inanimus: lifeless
incenatus: without dinner
incertus: uncertain; doubtful
incide (inc.): cut
incisus (inc. or **incis.)**: cut into pieces
incoctus: raw; uncooked
index [a sign]: the forefinger
indicaverit: it indicates; it shows
indicium (pl. **indicia**) [an indicating mark or sign]: a symptom
indies (ind.) or **in dies (in d.)**: daily
indolentia: free from pain
induratus: hardened
inedulis: inedible
infans: infant
infectorius: tainted
inferior: lower (in position or grade, as opposed to **superior**)
inferus: below; lower (as opposed to **superus**)
infestans: attacking; infesting
infestus: infested
infimus or **infumus**: lowest; the lowest part (as opposed to **summus**)
infirmitas: sickness

infirmus [weak or feeble]: sickly
inflammatio: inflammation
inflammatus: inflamed
inflatus: inflated
infra (**inf.**): below; underneath
infricetur (**infric.**): let it be rubbed in
infrons: leafless
infructuosus: fruitless; unproductive
infunde (**inf.**): pour in
infundibulum: a funnel
infuscatus: darkened
infusio or **infusum** (**inf.** or **infus.**): an infusion
infusus: infused
ingratus: ungrateful; disagreeable
inguen: the groin
inhalatio: an inhalation
inhaletur (**inhal.**): let it be inhaled
injectio (**inj.** or **inject.**): an injection
injectio hypodermica (**inj. hyp.**): hypodermic injection
injiciatur enema (**inj. enem.**): let an enema be injected
injuria: injury
innotatus: unmarked
innoxius: harmless
inodorus: odorless
inolens: without smell
inquietudo: restlessness
inquietus: restless
insanabilis: incurable
insanus: of unsound mind; insane
insequor or **insequitur**: to follow after, either in space or time
insipidus: tasteless
insomnia: sleeplessness
insomnis: sleepless
insomnitas: sleeplessness
inspiretur (**inspir.**): let it be breathed (into)
inspissatus: thickened
instanter: instantly; at once
instillentur (**instill.**): let them be dropped in or into
instilletur (**instill.**): let it be dropped in or into
insufflatio (**insuff.**): an insufflation

integer: whole; sound
inter: between; among
inter cenam: during dinner
inter cibos (i.c.): between meals
inter noctem (inter noct.): during the night
inter paroxysmos: between the attacks (i.e., the convulsions)
inter scapulas: between the shoulders
intercus: under the skin
interdum: now and then; sometimes
intermedius: intermediate
internus (int.): inward; internal
intestinalis: intestinal
intestinum: intestines; bowels
intime: intimately
intonsus: unshaven; with hair unshorn
intra: inside; within
intramuscularis: intramuscular
intus: inside; within
inula: elecampane or helenium plant
inunctio or **inunctum**: an inunction (i.e., an anointing)
invicem: by turns
involutum: rolled (up); wrapped
involve (involv.): roll; coat
iodatus: iodized
iodinium or **iodum (iod.)**: iodine
irradiatus: irradiated
iter a palato ad aureum: the path from the mouth to the ear (i.e., the Eustachian tube)
iteretur (iter.): let it be repeated
iterum: again; a second time
iterum atque iterum: again and again
iubatus or **jubatus**: having a mane (see also, **cristatus**)
iuglans or **juglans**: a walnut
iugulum or **jugulum**: the throat
iuxta or **juxta (iux.** or **jux.)**: near; next to

J

jam non: no more
jecunde: pleasantly

jecur or **iecur**: the liver (see also, **hepar**)
jentaculum or **ientaculum** (**jent.** or **jentac.**): breakfast
jubatus or **iubatus**: having a mane (see also, **cristatus**)
juglans or **iuglans**: a walnut
juglans regia: English walnut
juglans nigra: black walnut
jugulo (**jug.**): to or for the throat
jugulum or **iugulum**: the throat
julans: butternut
julepum or **julepus** or **julapium** (**jul.**): a julep
junceus [reedlike]: slender
junior: younger
juniperus: juniper
jus or **jusculum** (**jusc.**): juice; broth; soup
jus bovillum or **jus bovinum**: beef broth
jus gallinaceum: chicken broth
jus ovillum or **jusculum ovillum**: mutton broth
jus vitulinum: veal broth
jusculum avenaceum: gruel
juvenis: young; youthful
juventus (f. juventa): youth; adolescence; the prime of life
juxta or **iuxta** (**jux.** or **iux.**): near; next to

K

kali: potash
kali praeparatum: bicarbonate of potash
kalinus: containing potassium
kalium (**K.**): potassium
kaolinum: kaolin
keratinum: keratin
kilogramma (**kg.** or **kilo.** or **kilogra.**): kilogram
kilolitrum (**kl.**): kiloliter
kilometrum (**k.**): kilometer

L

labia or **labium**: lip; the lips
labia majora: the outer folds of the vulva
labia minora: the inner folds of the vulva

labium leporinum or **leporinum labium**: hare lip (i.e., a cleft lip)
labor or **laboris**: labor; work
lac: milk
lac bovinum: cow's milk
lac caprae: goat's milk
lac ovillum: sheep's milk
lac tepefactum: warmed milk
lac vaccae: cow's milk
lac vaccinum (**lac vac.**): cow's milk
lac vaccinum butyricum: buttermilk
lac vaccinum defloratum (**lac v.d.**) or **lac defloratum**: skimmed cow's milk
laceratio: tearing; mangling
lacerta: a lizard
lacertosus: muscular
lacertus: the upper arm with its muscles
lachesis: snake venom used in homeopathy
lacrima (pl. **lacrimae**): a tear
lactatus: lactated
lacticinium: foods prepared with milk
lacticus: lactic
lactosum: lactose
lactuca: garden lettuce (properly, **lactuca sativa**)
lactuca virosa: wild lettuce
lactucarium: lettuce juice (used as a sedative)
laetus: bright
laevigatus or **levigatus**: smoothed; polished; lightened
laevis or **levis**: smooth; light (in weight)
laevo: on the left
laevus (**laev.**): left
lagena: a bottle; flask
lamina [a thin plate or layer]: skin flakes; scales
lamina auri: gold leaf (see also, **auri lamina**)
lana: wool
laneus: woolen
languesco or **langui**: to be faint
languor: sickness
lanolinum: lanolin (see also, **adeps lanae**)
lapideus: of stone
lapis: stone

lapis calaminaris: calamine
lappa or **lappa officinalis**: burdock
lardum or **laridum**: lard
larix: the larch tree
lassus: weary
lateri dolenti (**lat. dol.**): to the painful side
latex: a fluid; a milky liquid of certain plants
Latine: in Latin
latissimus colli: the broad muscle of the neck
latissimus dorsi: the broad muscle of the back
latitudine (**lat.** or **latitud.**): in width
latus (**lat.**): side; flank; broad; wide
laudanum: tincture of opium
laurocerasus: cherry laurel
laurus: bay laurel
lavabrum: washing; a bath
lavandula: lavender
lavatio (**lavat.**): bathing; washing; also, a washing apparatus
laxans or **laxativus**: laxative
laxatus: loosened
laxus: loose; wide; spacious
leni calore: with gentle heat
leniens: soothing
lenis: gentle
leniter: gently
lenitivus: lenitive (i.e., a laxative)
lente: slowly
lentiginosus: freckled
lentigo: a freckle; a pimple
lentiscus: the mastic tree
lentus: tough; pliant; resistant
leontodon taraxacum or **taraxacum**: the dandelion (see also, **taraxacum dens-leonis**)
levator: a lifting muscle
levigatus or **laevigatus**: smoothed; polished; lightened
levis or **laevis**: smooth; light (in weight)
leviter: lightly
lex: law
liber: free
libitum: at pleasure

libra (lb.) [a pair of scales]: a Roman pound (i.e., 12 oz.); a U.S. pound (i.e., 16 oz.)
libra pondo (lb.): a pound by weight
licet: it is allowed
ligamenta subflava: the yellow ligaments that fill the spaces between the vertebrae
ligamentum: ligament; bandage
ligneus: wooden
lignum: wood
lilium candidum: white lily
limatura: filings
limetta: a lime
limon: lemon (see also, **citrus limonium**)
limpidus: limpid; clear
linctus (linct.): a soothing cough syrup
lineatus: lined; striped
lingua: the tongue
linimentum (lin.): a liniment
linimentum tempori applicandum: the liniment to be applied to the forehead
linteum or **linteola**: lint; linen
linteum carplum: lint
linteus: made of linen
linum: linseed; flaxseed
liquefactus: liquified
liquidum: liquid; a fluid
liquidus: flowing
liquor (liq.): liquor; fluid; solution
liquor amnii: amniotic fluid
liquor pancreatis: pancreatic fluid
liquor sanguinis: blood plasma
lithium (Li.): lithium
litrum (l. or **lit.)**: a liter
lobelia or **lobelia inflata**: Indian tobacco (see also, **tabacum**)
lobus: a lobe
localiter: locally
loco citato (loc. cit.): in the place cited
locum tenens (pl. **locum tenentes**): a substitute or deputy, especially for a physician or a cleric
locus: place

longicaudatus: long-tailed
longifolius: long-leaved
longissimus: the longest
longitudine (long.): in length
longus: long
longus colli: the long muscle of the neck
lotio (lot.): a lotion
lotio crinalis: hair lotion
lotus: washed
loxophthalmus: squinting of the eyes
lubricans: lubricating
lubricus: slippery
luce prima: early morning
lues: a plague; also, syphilis
lues venerea: syphilis
lumborum (sing. **lumbus**) (**lumb.**): the loins
lumbricus: worm
lumen: light
luminosus: luminous; glowing
luna: moon
lupulus: hops (see also, **humulus**)
lupus: wolf
luridus: pale yellow
luscinia: nightingale
lusus naturae: a freak of nature
luteus: of mud or clay; dirty
luteus: yellow-colored
lutum: clay
lux: light
luxus: dislocated
lycopersicum: a tomato
lycopodium: lycopodium; club moss
lympha: clear spring; river water

M

macera (mac.): macerate
macerare: to macerate (i.e., to soak)
macies: leanness; thinness
macilentus: thin; lean

macis or **macidis**: mace
macrocephalus: large-headed
macritudo: leanness
mactabilis: deadly; lethal
macula: spot; stain; blemish
macula matricis [spot from the mother]: a prenatal skin blemish
maculatus or **maculis distinctus**: spotted
madefactus: moistened
madidus: steeped; wet
magis minusve: more or less
magma magnesiae: milk of magnesia
magna cum cura: with great care
magnesiae sulphas or **magnesii sulphatis**: Epsom salt
magnus (**mag.**): large; great
major: larger; greater
mala: cheekbone or jawbone; the jaw or jaws
mala praxis [a bad practice]: malpractice
malae: cheeks
male positus (**m.p.** or **mal. pos.**): badly placed
malignus [hostile]: malignant
malleolus: ankle
malleolus internus: inner ankle
malleus: a hammer or mallet; a small bone of the inner ear
maltum: malt
malum: apple
malum medicum: an ancient name for a lemon (also, **malum citrium**)
malum punicum [Phoencian apple]: a pomegranate
malus: bad
malva: the mallow plant
mamillosus: pertaining to the breasts
mamma or **mamilla**: breast; teat
mammalia: mammals
mancus: crippled; maimed
mandibula: the lower jaw (see also, **maxilla inferior**)
mandragora: mandrake; the may apple (see also, **podophyllum**)
mane (**m.**): morning; in the morning
mane et nocte (**m. et n.**): morning and night
mane et vespere (**m. et v.**): morning and evening
mane primo (**m.p.** or **m. pr.** or **m. prim.**): early in the morning
mane sequenti (**m. seq.**): on the following morning

manet cicatrix: the scar remains
manganum: manganese
mania: madness
mania a potu [mania from drinking]: delirium tremens
manipulus: a handful
manna: formerly, a laxative derived from the European ash tree
manu calefacta: with a warm hand
manu scriptum (**m.s.** or **ms.**): written by hand (i.e., a manuscript)
manubrium [handle]: a part of the sternum
manus: hand
manus aversa: the back of the hand
manus dextra: the right hand
manus sinistra (or simply, **sinistra**): the left hand
mare: the sea
marginalis: marginal
margo: margin; border; edge
maritimus: marine
maritus: a husband
marrubium: horehound
marsupium: a pouch (e.g., the scrotum)
mas or **masculus** (**m.**): male; a man
masculinus or **masculinum** (**m.** or **masc.**): masculine; manly
massa (**mas.** or **mass.**): a mass
massa pilularum (**m.p.**): a pill mass
masticare: to chew
mastiche: mastic
mater: mother
materia: material
materia medica [medical material]: the body of collected knowledge concerning the various notions and remedies used by physicians to heal patients, including their nature, properties, and standard preparations
matrix: mother; the womb
maturus: ripe; mature
matutinus (**matut.**): of the morning
maxilla: jaw; the upper jaw
maxilla inferior: the lower jaw (see also, **mandibula**)
maxime: chiefly; mostly
maximus: the greatest; the largest
mays or **maydis**: corn; maize (see also, **zea mays**)

meatus: a cavity; an opening; a passage
meatus auritorius: the ear passage
meatus urinarius: the urethra
media nocte: in the middle of the night
medicabilis: curable
medicago: alfalfa; lucerne
medicamen or **medicamentum**: a drug or medicine
medicamentarius: a pharmacist; a druggist
medicatus: medicated; drugged
Medicinae Doctor (M.D.): Doctor of Medicine
medicinalis: medicinal
medicinus (medicina): medicine (i.e., the art of healing)
medicus: healing; medicinal; also, a physician
medicus auricularius: an ear doctor
medicus chirurgus: a surgeon
medicus ludi: doctor of the games (i.e., a sports doctor)
medicus ocularius: an eye doctor
Medicus Veterinarius (M.V.): Doctor of Veterinarian Science
mediocris: mediocre; middling; of indifferent quality
mediocritas: moderation
medius: medium; middle-sized
medulla: pith; marrow
medulla oblongata: the lower part of the brain, continuous with the spinal cord
medulla spinalis: the spinal cord
mel: honey
mel despumatum: clarified honey
meliferus: honey-producing
melilotus: sweet clover
melior: better
melissa officinalis: lemon balm
membrana: membrane
membrana tympani: the membrane of the ear drum
membratim [limb by limb]: one by one; piecemeal
membrum: limb
membrum virile [the male member]: the penis
memento [remember]: a memorandum
memor: mindful; remembering
menispermum: moonseed
mens: mind

menses: period of menstruation
mensis: month
menstruum: a solvent
menstruus: monthly; monthlong
mensura (**mens.** or **mensur.**): measure; by measure
mentha: mint
menthae alcohol: menthol
mentha piperita: peppermint (see also, **piperita**)
mentha pulegium or **pulegium**: pennyroyal
mentha viridis: spearmint
menthol: menthol (supposedly a contraction of **menthae alcohol**)
mentum: the chin
mephitis: a foul-smelling gas or odor
merda: excrement
meridiatio: a midday nap; a siesta
meridies: midday; noon
merum: pure or unmixed wine
merus: pure; undiluted; unadulterated
mesogastrium: the central area of the abdomen
metallicus: metallic
metallum: metal
metrum (**m.**): a meter
mica: crumb; morsel
mica panis (**mic. pan.**): bread crumb
micrococcus: a small berry
mictus: urinating
mictus cruentus: bloody urine (see also, **sanguinis mictus**)
mille (pl. **millia**): one thousand
milligramma: milligram
millilitrum: milliliter
mineralis: mineral
minimum (**m.** or **min.**): a minim; a drop; a very small amount
minimus: smallest; least
minor: smaller
minus: less
minutum or **minutus** (**minut.**): a minute or small amount
misce (**m.** or **M.**): mix
misce, detur, signetur (**m.d.s.**): mix, give, sign
misce fiant pilulae (**m. ft. pil.**): mix to make or form pills
misce fiat mistura (**m. ft. m.**): mix to make a mixture

misce fiat pulvis (m. ft. p.): mix to make a powder
misce secundum artem (m.s.a.): mix according to practice
misceantur: let them be mixed
miscet (pl. **miscent**): he or she mixes
misericordia: mercy; compassion
mistura (mist.): a mixture
mistura acida: the acid mixture
misturae sequentis: of the following mixture
mitigatus: mitigated (i.e., reduced in strength); relieved
mitis: mild
mittatur (pl. **mittantur**; **mitt.** or **mittr.**): let it be sent; let it be drawn
mittatur sanguis (mitt. sang.): let blood be drawn
mitte (mitt.): send
mitte tales (mitt. tal. or **mit. tal.)**: send such
mixtum compositum: a hodgepodge
mixtus: mixed
modicissimus: a very little
modicus: moderate-sized; middle-sized
modo dicto (mod. dict.): as written; as prescribed
modo praescripto (mod. praesc. or **mod. praes.)**: in the manner prescribed
modulus: a mold
modus: manner; way
moles: weight; mass
molestante dolore: the pain being troublesome
molestante tussi: the cough being troublesome
molestia or **molestus**: irksome; troublesome
mollis: soft
mollities cerebri: softening of the brain
mollities ossium: softening of the bones
mons veneris: the female pubic region
montanus: of the mountain
mora: delay
morbilli: the measles (i.e., **rubeola**)
morbillosus: pertaining to the measles
morbo corripi: racked with disease
morbus: sickness; disease
morbus caducas [falling sickness]: epilepsy
morbus comitialis: epilepsy
morbus coxarius: disease of the hip or hip joint

morbus ingravescit: the disease grows worse
morbus virgineus [virgin's disease]: chlorosis (both being early modern terms for hypochronic anemia, that is, iron deficiency, experienced by young women)
morbus vulpis: alopecia (see also, **vulpis morbus**)
mordicus [by biting]: with the teeth
more dicto (**m.d.** or **more dict.**): as directed; in the manner directed
more solito (**m.s.** or **more sol.**): in the usual manner
moribundus: dying; on the verge of death
morphina: morphine
morrhua: codfish
morrhuae oleum: cod liver oil
mors: death
mors immatura or **mors praematura**: a premature or untimely death
morsus: a bite
mortalis: mortal
mortario aheneo: in a brass or iron mortar
mortario marmoreo: in a marble mortar
mortario vitreo: in a glass mortar
mortarium: a mortar
mortuus: dead
mos (pl. **mores**): custom; manner
moschiferus: musk-bearing
moschus: musk
motores oculorum: the nerves that move the eyes
mox: soon
mucidus: moldy; musty
mucilago (**muc.** or **mucil.**): mucilage
muciparus: mucus-producing
mucus: mucus
muliebris: of a woman; also, a wife
mulier: a woman
mulla: mull; salve mull
multicavus: porous
multus: much; many
muriaticus: muriatic; hydrochloric
murus: wall
mus: a mouse or rat
musca: a fly

muscae volitantes [flying flies]: a type of vision impairment in which one sees faint objects flying or floating before the eyes (see also, **flocci volitantes** or flying specks)
musculus: muscle
muticus: docked; curtained
mutilus: maimed; mutilated
mutitas atonica: nerve defect of the tongue resulting in the inability to speak
mutitas sudorum: the inability to speak due to deafness
mutus: mute
myrica acris: the source of bay rum
myristica: nutmeg (properly, **myristica moschata**)
myrrha: myrrh (see also, **balsamodendron myrrha**)
myrtum: myrtle berry
myrtus: myrtle tree
mystus: whiskered

N

naevius: having spots or moles
naevus: a mole
naevus maternus [maternal marks]: a birthmark (i.e., a mark on the neck of a child at birth)
nanus: a dwarf
napellus: a small turnip
naris (pl. **nares**): the nose; a nostril
narthecium: a gallipot (i.e., a pharmacist's medicine or ointment jar)
naso: to or for the nose
nasoguttae: nose drops
nasus (pl. **nasi**): the nose; also, the sense of smell
nates: the buttocks
natans: floating
natrium (**Na.**): sodium
natu: by birth
naturalia: the sex organs
naturalis: natural
natus (**n.**): born
nausea: general nausea
nausea marina: seasickness
ne: lest; not

ne admittas: do not admit
ne nimis: not too much
ne repetatur (**ne rep.**): do not repeat
ne tradas sine nummo (**n.t.s.n.** or **ne tr. s. num.**): do not deliver unless paid (i.e., c.o.d.)
nebula (**nebul.**): a mist or vapor; a spray
nemino contradicenti: no one contradicting
nemo: no man; no one
neonatus: newly born
nepa: a scorpion (see also, **scorpio**)
nepeta cataria: catnip; catmint
nequam: worthless
nervus: nerve; sinew
neuter: neither; of neither sex
neutralis: neutral
nevus or **naevus**: birthmark
nidus: nest
niger (**nig.**): black
nigrobaccus: blackberry
nihil or **nil**: nothing
nil per os (**n.p.o.**): nothing by mouth
nimis: very much; too much
nisi: unless
nisus: straining or exertion; the action of the diaphragm and abdominal muscles in expelling any matter from the body (e.g., feces, urine, vomit)
nisus formativus: the vital power in the organs of the body to perform their specific functions
nitidus: bright; glossy; also, blooming; flourishing
nitras: nitrate
nitricus: nitric
nitris: nitrite
nitrogenium: nitrogen
nitroglycerinum: nitroglycerine
nitrosus: nitrous
nitrum: soda
nivalis or **niveus**: snowy; snowy white
nix: snow
nocte (**n.**): at night; in the night
nocte et mane (**n. et m.**): night and morning

nocte maneque (**n.m.**): night and morning
noctes: nights
noctu: by night
nocturnus: nocturnal; by night
nodulo ligati: tied with a knot
nodulus: a little knot
nodus: a knot; a node
noli me tangere [touch me not]: historically referring to skin diseases, such as lupus
nomen (pl. **nomina**; **nom.**): name
nomen proprium (**n.p.** or **N.P.**): proper name
nomen specificum ex nomine vulgari depromptum: the specific (or species) name taken from the common name
non: no
non compos mentis: not of sound mind
non dolet: it does not hurt
non licet (**n.l.**): it is not permitted
non liquet: it does not melt
non repetatur (**non rep.**): let it not be repeated (i.e., do not refill)
nonaginta: ninety
nondum natus: unborn
nongenti: nine hundred
nonus: the ninth
nostrum: quack medicine
nota bene (**N.B.** or **n.b.**): note well
novem: nine
novus: new
nox (pl. **noctes**): night
nucha or **nucha capitis** (**nuch. cap.**): the nape of the neck
nucleus: a pit or stone
nudatum corpus: the naked body
nudus: bare; naked
nullum datum: no date
nullus: no; none
numero (**No.** or **no.**): in number; by number; to the number of
numerus: number
nummus: money
nutans: nodding (in approval)
nutriens: nourishing
nutrimen or **nutrimentum**: nourishment

nutrix: a child's nurse
nux (pl. **nuces**): a nut
nux Gallica [Gallic nut]: a walnut
nux moschata: nutmeg
nux vomica: Quaker button (used as a heart stimulant)
nymphae odorata: the water lily

O

obduce: coat; cover
obducere: to coat
obesus: fat; swollen
obiit (ob.): he or she died
oblatum (oblat.): a cachet (e.g., a medicine capsule)
obscuro loco natus: of unknown origin
obscurus: dark; dull; obscure
obsoletus: obsolete; worn out
obstetrix: a midwife
obturatus: stoppered; closed
obtusifolius: blunt-leaved
occidentalis: occidental; western
occiput: the back of the head (as opposed to **sinciput**)
octarius (O or **oct.)**: a pint
octavus: the eighth
octo: eight
octoginta: eighty
oculentum: an eye ointment
oculi uterque (o.u.): for both eyes
oculo arte adjuto: with a lens
oculoguttae: eye drops
oculus (pl. **oculi**): the eye
oculus dexter (o.d.): the right eye
oculus sinister (o.s.): the left eye
odontalgia: a toothache
odontalgia urgente: with the toothache being most troublesome
odontalgicum: toothache drops
odor: odor; a smell
odoratus: odorous
officialis: official; approved
officinalis: authorized for use in an apothecary shop

oleatus: oiled
oleosaccharum: oil sugar (see also, **elaeosaccharum**)
oleosus: oily
oleum (**ol.**): oil
oleum jecoris aselli: cod liver oil
oleum olivae (**o.o.** or **ol. ol.**): olive oil (see also, **olivum**)
oleum succini: oil of amber
olfactus: sense of smell
olibanum: frankincense
oliva: olive
olivum: olive oil (see also, **oleum olivae**)
olla: a jar
olla fictilis: earthenware jar
omne die (**o.d.** or **omn. die**): all day; every day
omne scibile: everything knowable
omni alterna hora (**o. alt. h.**): every other hour
omni biduo: every two days
omni bihora or **omni bihorio** (**o.b.** or **omn. bih.**): every two hours
omni hora (**o.h.** or **omn. hor.**): every hour
omni mane (**o.m.** or **omn. man.**): every morning
omni nocte (**o.n.** or **omn. noc.**): every night
omni quadranta hora (**o.q.h.** or **omn. quad. hor.**): every quarter hour (i.e., every fifteen minutes)
omni sexta hora (**o. sext. h.**): every six hours
omni singula hora (**o.s.h.** or **o. sing. h.**): every single hour
omni triduo: every three days
omnibus alternis horis (**omn. alt. hor.**): every other hour; at alternate hours
omnis (**omn.**): all; every
opacus: dark; shaded; shadowy; obscure
ope: by means of
ope bacilli lignei: by means of a small wooden stick
ope cribri: by means of or through a sieve
ope penicilli (**ope pen.**): by means of a camel-hair brush
opere citato (**op. cit.**): in the work cited
opertus: covered
ophthalmia neonatorum: the optic nerve
ophthalmicus: ophthalmic (pertaining to the eye)
opprobrium medicorum [the reproach of physicians]: an incurable disease

opticus: optic
optimus (**opt.**): the best
opulus: maple tree
opus (pl. **opera**): work; need; occasion
opus est: it is necessary
orbicularis oris: the lip muscle (see also, **constrictor oris**)
orbicularis palpebrarum: the muscle that shuts the eye
orbis: circle
ordinarius: ordinary
ori: to or for the mouth
orientalis: oriental; eastern
origanum: marjoram
ornus: mountain ash tree
oryza: rice
os (pl. **ora**): the mouth; an opening
os (pl. **ossa**): a bone
os externus: the mouth of the vagina
os femoris: the femur bone
os humeri: the humerus bone (i.e., upper arm)
os innominatum: the hip bone
os jugale: the cheekbone (see also, **zygoma**)
os malare or **os malae**: the cheekbone (see also, **zygoma**)
os pectoris: the breastbone; the sternum
os sepiae: cuttlefish bone
os tincae: the mouth of the womb
os ustum: bone ash
os uteri or **os internum**: the mouth of the uterus
os zygomaticum: the cheekbone (see also, **zygoma**)
oscillatio: swinging to and fro
osculum: a small mouth or opening (also, a kiss)
ossa [bones]: a skeleton
ossa pubis: the pubic bone
osseus: bony
ossicula: small bones
ossium compages: the skeletal system
ostium: an opening
ostrea: oyster
otoguttae: ear drops
ovarium: ovary
ovatus: egg-shaped

ovi albumen (**ovi alb.**): the egg white
ovi putamen: an egg shell
ovi vitellus (**ovi vit.**) or **vitellus**: the egg yolk (see also, **vitellus ovi**)
ovillum jusculum (**ovil. jus.**): mutton broth
ovillus: pertaining to sheep
ovis: a sheep
ovorum: of eggs
ovula: an ovule
ovum (**ov.**): an egg
oxidatus: oxidized
oxidum: oxide
oxygenium: oxygen
oxymel (**ox.** or **oxy.** or **oxym.**): a mixture of honey, vinegar, and water
oxyuris vermicularis: the tapeworm

P

pabulum: food
paene: nearly; almost
palatum: the palate (i.e., the roof of the mouth)
palatum durum [hard palate]: the front of the mouth
palatum molle [soft palate]: the back part of the mouth
pallidulus: somewhat pale
pallidus: pale; sallow
palma: the palm of the hand
palmatus: palmlike
palmus: the width of the hand
palmus major: the span of the hand
palmus minor: the width of four fingers (i.e., the width of the hand minus the thumb)
palpebra: the eyelid
paluster: swampy
panacea [a plant believed to heal all ailments]: a cure-all
panax quiquefolius: American ginseng
panchrestus: good or useful for everything
pancreaticus: pancreatic
panis: bread
panis azymus: unleavened bread
panis mica: a bread crumb
panniculus: a covering

pannus: cloth; rag
pannus laneus: a woolen flannel cloth
pannus linteus: a linen cloth
papaver: poppy
papaver somniferum: the poppy from which opium and morphine are derived
papilla (pl. **papillae**): nipple; teat
papula: a pimple
pappus: the first soft beard on the chin
paraffinum: paraffin
paradoxus: paradoxic; uncharacteristic
paralysis agitans: Parkinson's disease
paratus: prepared; ready
parens: a parent
paries (pl. **parietis**): a side or wall of a cavity
paroxysmus: a paroxysm (i.e., a fit); convulsion
pars (pl. **partes**): part
partem affectam (part. aff.): affected part
partem dolentem (part. dolent.): painful part
partes aequales (p. ae. or **pt. aeq.**): in equal parts
partes constituentes: constituent parts (i.e., the ingredients)
parti affectae (p.a.): to the affected part
parti dolenti (p. dol.): to the painful part
parti affectae applicandus (p.a.a.): to be applied to the affected part
parti affectae pingendus: to be painted on the affected part
partiat: let him or her divide
partibus affectis (p.a.): to the affected parts
partitio: a division; partition
partitis vicibus (part. vic.): in divided doses
partitus: divided
partus: birth; giving birth
parum: too little; not enough
parum profuit: it (the cure) helped too little; or, it helped for a little while
parumper: for a little while
parviflorus: small-flowered
parvulum [very little]: a little bit
parvulus [very small]: a little one (i.e., an infant)
parvus (parv.): small
pasta: a paste

passiflora: passion flower
passim (pass.): throughout; here and there
passulae: raisins (see also, **uvae passae**)
pastillum or **pastillus (pas.** or **pastil.)**: a small lozenge; a breath lozenge
pastinaca: the parsnip (properly, **pastinaca sativa**)
pastus: food
patella: the kneecap
patens: open; accessible
pater: father
patiens: a patient
patina: an evaporating dish
pauciflorus: having few flowers
pauculum: a little
paucus: a little
paulatim: little by little
paulum or **paullum (paul.)**: a little
paulum cibi gustandum: a little food is to be taken
paululus or **paululum**: very little
pauxillum (paux.): a very little
pectinum: pectin
pectoralis: pectoral; also, an expectorant
pectori (pect.): to the chest or breast
pectus (pect.): the chest; breast
pedetentim (pedet.): step by step; by degrees
pediculus: louse
pediculus pubis: the crab louse
pediluvium: a foot bath
pedis digitus: a toe
peior or **pejor**: worse
peius or **pejus**: even worse
pellis: skin; hide
peltatus: shield-like
pelvis [a basin]: the pelvic region
pendens (pend.): weighing; hanging
penicillum: a brush; also, a pencil
penicillum camelinum (pen. cam. or **penicul. cam.)**: a camel's hair brush
penicillum pro gutture: a brush for the throat
peniculus: a brush; a sponge
penis [tail]: the male sex organ (see also, **membrum virile**)
penitus: inward; internal

penna: a feather
pennatus: winged; feathered
pensus: weighted
pepo: a pumpkin (see also, **cucurbita pepo**)
pepsinum: pepsin
pepticus: digestive
peptonatus: peptonized
per biduum: for two days
per cribrum trajicere: to pass through a sieve
per deliquium: by deliquescence
per diem [by the day]: daily
per fistulam: through a tube
per horam [by the hour]: for an hour
per infortunium: by accident
per mensem [by the month]: monthly; for each month
per os (p.o.): by mouth; orally
per saltum (per salt.): by leaps; all at once
per se: by itself
per singulos dies: day by day; every day
per somnum: asleep
per tres consequentes noctes: for three consecutive nights
per triduum: for three days
per vicem: by turns; alternately
per vim: by force; forcibly
peractus: completed
peracta operatione emetici: the emetic having completed its action (i.e., the emetic having acted)
percolet: let it percolate
percolatum: percolate
percolum: percolator
perendie: on the day after tomorrow
perfoliatus: having a stem passing through the leaf
perforatus: pierced
perfricandus: to be rubbed
perfricetur: let it be rubbed
pergat in usu medicinarum: let the patient continue using the medicine
pergat in usu remediorum: let the patient continue using the remedy
peritus: skilled
peroxidum: peroxide

perpallidus: very pale
perpolitio: a polishing
persiccus: very dry
persio: cudbear (i.e., a purple dye)
perstetur (**P.** or **pt.**): let it be continued
pertussis: whooping cough (see also, **tussis convulsiva**)
pervigilium: inability to sleep
pes or **pedis** (pl. **pedes**): the foot
pessimus: worst
pessus (**pess.**): a pessary; a vaginal suppository
pestis: a pest; plague or pestilence; a contagious fever
petalum (pl. **petala**): a petal
petra: rock; stone
petrolatum: petroleum jelly (see also, **vaselinum**)
petroleum [rock oil]: petroleum oil
petroselinum: parsley
phagedaenicus: cancerous; spreading like cancer
pharmaceuticus: pharmaceutical
Pharmaciae Doctor [**Phar. D.** or **Pharm. D.**]: Doctor of Pharmacy
pharmacopoeia: a pharmacopoeia (i.e., an official book listing medicines with their uses and effects)
pharmacopola: a druggist; also, a quack
phellus: a cork
phiala [phial]: vial; bottle
phiala agitata: the bottle having been shaken
phiala bene obturata: a well-sealed bottle
phiala obturata: a sealed or stoppered bottle
phiala prius agitata (**p.p.a.** or **P.P.A.**): after first shaking the bottle
phiala prius concussa: the bottle having been previously shaken
phiala suberata: a corked bottle
Philosophiae Doctor (**Ph.D.**): Doctor of Philosophy
philtrum (pl. **philtra**): a love potion
philtrum: the vertical groove or indented space between the nose and the upper lip (colloquially, Cupid's bow)
phlegmasia cerulea dolens: deep-vein thrombosis (i.e., a blood clot)
phosphas: phosphate
phosphoricus: phosphoric
phosphorosus: phosphorous
phosphorus: phosphorus

phrenesis: madness; frenzy
phthisis: consumption (i.e., tuberculosis)
physica: physics
physiologicus: physiological
physostigma: Calabar bean
phytolacca: poke root
picea: pitch pine
piceus: of or like pitch; pitch-black
pictus: painted
pigmentum (pigm.): pigment; paint
pila: ball
pilocarpus: jaborandi (the leaves of the **pilocarpus pinnatus**)
pilorum arrectores: the tiny muscles that produce the 'goose bumps' effect as well as the skin hair to rise when a person is cold or frightened
pilosus: covered with hair; hairy
pilula (pl. **pilulae**; **pil.**): a pill
pilulae tunicatae: coated pills
pilum: a pestle
pilum ligneum: a wooden pestle
pilus: hair
pimenta dioica: allspice
pimpinella: anise (properly, **pimpinella asinum**)
pinguedo: lard; fat; grease
pinguis: plump; fatty; greasy
pinus: pine
piper: pepper
piper nigrum: black pepper
piperita: peppermint (see also, **mentha piperita**)
piperitus: peppery
pirus or **pyrus**: pear
piscarius: related to fish
piscina: a fish tank; a fish pond; also, a swimming pond
piscis: fish
pistachium: the pistachio fruit
pistillum: a pestle (see also, **pilum**)
pisum (pl. **pisa**): the pea
pix: pitch
pix carbonis: coal tar
pix liquida: tar; wood tar

pix lithanthracis: coal tar paste
placabilis: easy to please
placebo (. . .): I will please (i.e., a prescription given to please a patient)
placidus: quiet; still
planifolius: flat-leaved
planta: the sole of the foot
plantago: plantain
planum: plain; intelligible
planum facere: to make plain; to explain
planus: flat; level
plasma: the fluid part of blood; also, a non-fatty ointment made of starch and gylcerin
plenus: plenty; full; complete
plexus: braid; network; a network of blood vessels or nerves
plica: a fold; a plait
plico: to fold together
ploratus: weeping; crying; to weep over or lament
pluma: feather
plumatus: covered with feathers
plumosum: feathered
plumbum (Pb. or pb.): lead
plumbum album [white lead]: tin
plumeus: downy
pluries: frequently; often
plurimus: most
plus: more
pluvia: rain
pluvialis: pertaining to rain; sprouting after the rain
pluvialis aqua: rainwater
pocillum (pocill.): a small cup
poculum (poc. or **pocul.)**: a cup
podagra: gout in the feet
podex: anus; anal region; buttocks
podophyllum: may apple; mandrake (see also, **mandragora**)
pollen [fine flour]: pollen (i.e., the powder found in flowers that possesses regenerative power)
pollex (poll.): the thumb or big toe; an inch in length
pollices sex (poll. sex): six inches (i.e., half a foot)
pomadum: a pomade
pomatus: pertaining to apples

pomeridianus: of the afternoon
pomifer: fruit-bearing
pomum: an apple
pomum Adami: the Adam's apple
pondere (**P.**): by weight
ponderosus: heavy; weighty
pondus: weight
pondus medicinale: an apothecary's weight
pondus specificum: a specific weight
pone aurem (**pone aur.**): put behind the ear
pone in capsulas: put in capsules
pons (pl. **pontes**) [a bridge]: a part connecting two other parts
populus: the poplar tree
porca: a sow
porcus: a hog
porrigo: dandruff; ringworm of the scalp
porta: a gate
portentus: indicated; predicted; foretold
portio: part; portion; section
portio dura: the facial nerve
portio mollis: the auditory nerve
porus: a pore; a callus
positus: position; place
post: after
post cibos (**p.c.**): after meals
post cibum (**p.c.**): after food
post duas horas: after two hours
post jentaculum (**p.j.** or **p. jent.** or **p. jentac.**): after breakfast
post meridianus or **postmeridianus**: in or of the afternoon
post meridiem (**p.m.** or **P.M.**): after noon
post mortem (**p.m.** or **P.M.**): after death
post obitum: after death
post partum or **postpartum**: after birth
post postscriptum (**P.P.S.** or **PPS**): an additional postscript
post prandium: after dinner
post scriptum or **postscriptum** (**P.S.** or **PS**): written after; a postscript
post singulas dejectiones liquidas (**p.s.d.l.**): after each loose bowel movement
post singulas sedes liquidas (**p.s.s.l.**): after each loose stool
postea: thereafter; afterwards; next

posterior: at the rear; the rear part
postridie: on the following day
potassa: potash
potassium (K.): potassium
potens: strong; powerful
potestas res cognoscendi: the power of the recognition of things
potio or **potus (pot.)**: a potion; a drink; a draught
prae manu: at hand; on hand
praecipitatus (ppt.): precipitated
praecox: premature
praemolior: to prepare beforehand
praenomen: first name
praeparatio: preparation
praeparatus (praep.): prepared
praeparetur: let it be prepared
praeparentur: let them be prepared
praescriptio or **praescriptum** [precept or rule]: something prescribed; a prescription
praesentia animi: presence of mind
prandium (prand.): lunch or dinner
pratum: a meadow
pratensis [of a meadow]: growing in a meadow
prelum: a press
pressus: pressure
prima luce (prim. luc.) [at first light]: early in the morning
primae viae: the primary passages of the body (e.g., the stomach and the intestines)
primipara: a mother who is pregnant with or has delivered her first child
primo mane (prim. m.): early in the morning
primus: the first
princeps: prince; principal; first
pristinus: former; earlier
prius: coming before, prior, previous
pro: for; before; on behalf of
pro adulto: for an adult
pro capillis (pro capill.): for the hair
pro dose: for a dose
pro dosi: as or for a dose
pro jugulo (pro jug.): for the throat

pro lubitu: according to desire
pro naso: for the nose
pro oculis (pro ocul.): for the eyes
pro oculo dextro (pro ocul. dext.): for the right eye
pro oculo laevo (pro ocul. laev.): for the left eye
pro portione: in proportion
pro potu communi: for an ordinary drink
pro potu sumendus (pro pot. s.): to be taken as a drink
pro ratione aetatis (p.r.a. or **pro rat. aet.)**: according to age of the patient
pro ratione doloris: according to the pain
pro re nata (p.r.n. or **P.R.N.)**: whenever necessary; as needed
pro singulis oculis (pro sing. ocul.): for each eye
pro tempore (p.t. or pro tem.): for a time; temporarily
pro usu externo: for external use
pro recto (pro rect.): rectal
pro vagina (pro vagin.): vaginal
pro urethra (pro ureth.): urethral
procumbens: prostrate (i.e., lying on the ground)
profluens: running water
profundus: deep-seated
prolapsus: a collapse or falling; a protrusion
prolapsus ani: a collapse or falling of the extremity of the anus
prolapsus uteri: a collapse or falling of the womb
prope: near
proprius [one's own]: proper; suitable
prosum: to be useful; to benefit someone or something
proteinum: protein
protinus: instantly
proxima luce: the next day; also, the day before
proximo (prox.): the next; of or in the following month
proximo mense (prox. m.): the next month
proximus: the closest or nearest
prudentia: prudence; discretion
pruina: hoarfrost; rime
pruna: a live or burning coal
prunum: a plum or prune
prunus: plum tree
prunus serotina: wild cherry (also, **prunus virginiana**)
pruriens: itching

prurigo: itch (i.e., a skin eruption attended by itching)
pruritus: an itching; excessive itching
psora: the itch
puberulus: having soft short hairs
pubescens: pubescent
pudenda muliebre: the female reproductive system
pudenda virorum: the male reproductive system
puella: a girl; a female youth
puer: a boy; a male youth
puerpera: a woman in labor
puerperium: childbirth; labor
pugillus (pug.): a pinch (i.e., the amount that can be grasped by two or three fingers)
pugnus: the fist
pulegium: pennyroyal (see also, **mentha pulegium**)
pulex: a flea
pullus: a chicken
pulmentum: a relish
pulmo (pl. **pulmones**): a lung
pulpa: fruit pulp
puls: a porridge; pottage made of grain
pulsatilis: a throbbing headache
pulsatio: a knocking or beating of something
pulsus: pulse
pulsus cordis: the beat of the heart
pulveratus: pulverized
pulveres (pulv.): powders
pulvereus: powdery
pulverisatus: powdered
pulvis (pulv.): a powder
pulvis conspersus (pulv. consper.): a dusting powder
pulvis subtilis: a fine powder
pulvis subtilissimus: a very fine powder; the very finest powder
pumex: pumice
pumilio or **pumilus**: a dwarf
puncta lachrymalia: the openings in the lower eyelids where the tears form or appear
punctatus: pointed; spotted
punctum: point; spot; moment
punctum caecum: the blind spot of the eye

punctum saliens: the first movement of the embryo after fertilization
punica granatum or **punica**: the pomegranate
purgans: purging; laxative
purgatio alvi: purging of the bowels; a laxative
purgativus: a purgative
purgus: purgative; purging
purificatus: purified; refined
purpureus: purple
purus: pure
pustula: a blister; a pimple
putridus: rotten; decayed
putris: rotten; putrid
putus: pure; unmixed
pygmaeus: dwarf-sized
pyorrhea alveolaris: Rigg's disease
pyramidalis: pyramid-shaped
pyrus or **pirus**: pear tree
pyxis (pyx.): a pill box
pyxis chartacea: a powder box

Q

qua: which; as far as
quacumque: in whatever way
quadraginta: forty
quadrans: a quarter; a fourth part
quadratus: squared
quadringenti: four hundred
quadrupes: four-footed
quadruplex: quadruple
quae vide (qq.v.): (pl.) which see
quaeque: each; every
quaestio or **questio**: a question; an inquiry
qualus: a wicker basket
quam: as much as; than
quam maxime: as much as possible
quam multi?: how many?
quamdiu: as long as; so long as; until
quamdiu?: for how long?
quamlibet: as much as you please

quamprimum: as soon as possible
quamvis or **quam vis**: as much as you will; however much
quantitas (**qt.**): quantity
quantitas duplex (**qt. dupx.** or **qt. dx.**): twice the quantity (i.e., double the amount)
quantulus: how little; how small
quantum: as much as
quantum libet (**q.l.** or **q. lib.**): as much as you please; liberally
quantum placet (**q. pl.** or **q.p.**): as much as you please; agreeably
quantum satis (**q.s.** or **Q.S.**): as much as satisfies
quantum sufficit or **quantum sufficiat** (**q.s.** or **quant. suff.**): as much as suffices
quantum vis or **quantumvis** (**q.v.**): as much as you will
quantum volueris (**q. vol.** or **q.v.**): as much as you wish
quantus: how much?
quantus: how great; how much; how many
quaque (**qq.** or **Qq.**): each; every
quaque alterna hora (**q. alt. h.**): every other hour
quaque hora (**q.h.** or **qq. hor.**): every hour
quaque mane (**q.m.** or **Q.M.**): every morning
quaque nocte (**q.n.**): every night
quaque sexta hora (**q. sext. h.**): every six hours
quaque singula hora (**q.s.h.** or **q. sing. h.**): every single hour
quarta pars: a quarter part; one quarter
quartana or **febris quartana**: a fever occurring every fourth day, as in malaria
quartis horis (**quart. hor.**): every four hours
quartus: the fourth
quarum or **quorum**: of which; of whom
quasi: as if; as though; as it were
quasi dicat (**q.d.**): as much as to say
quasi dictum (**q.d.**): as if said
quasillus or **quasillum**: a little basket
quatenus: how far; in so far as; to what extent
quater: four times
quater die (**q.d.**): four times a day
quater in die (**q.i.d.**): four times a day
quaterni: four each; four at a time
quattuor or **quatuor**: four
quattuordecim: fourteen

quercus: oak
quibus: from which; with which
quies: rest; repose
quiescat: let him or her be still; let him or her rest
quietus: quiet; calm; still
quillaja: the soap or soapbark tree (properly, **quillaja saponaria**)
quindecim: fifteen
quinina: quinine
quingenti: five hundred
quinquaginta: fifty
quinque: five
quinquies: five times
quinquies vel sexies in die (**quin. vel sex. in d.**): five or six times a day
quintus: the fifth
quisque: each one; every one
quod: which; that; because
quod erat demonstrandum (**Q.E.D.** or **q.e.d.**): which was to be demonstrated or proven
quod erat faciendum (**Q.E.F.** or **q.e.f.**): which was to be done
quod est (**q.e.**): which is
quod superest: the remainder
quod vide (**q.v.**): (sing.) which see
quomodo: in what manner or way
quoque (**qq.** or **Qq.**): also; too
quorum or **quarum**: of which; of whom
quotannis: annually
quotidianus: daily; every day
quotidie (**quot.** or **quotid.**): daily; every day
quoties: as often as; whenever
quoties opus sit (**q.o.s.** or **quot. op. sit**): as often as required
quotquot: as many as

R

rabies: madness
racemosus: clustered (i.e., having racemes)
raditicus: by the roots
radius: ray
radix: a root
ramenta: shavings; splinters; chips

ramulus: a small branch
ramus: branch
rana: frog
rapa or **rapum**: turnip
rapulum: a small turnip
raspatus: rasped
rasurae eboris: ivory shavings
rasuratus: scraped
rasus: shaved; shredded; trimmed
ratio: ratio; proportion
raucitas: hoarseness
raucitate urgente: with hoarseness being serious
recens (rec.): recent; fresh
recipe (R): take
recuperatio: recovery
rectalis: rectal
rectificatus: rectified; refined
rectum intestinum or **rectum**: the rectum, specifically the lower section of the intestines
rectus: straight; right; correct
rectus abdominis: the abdominal muscles
rectus femoris: the thigh muscles
rectus musculus: any of various straight muscles
redactus: reduced
redestillatus: redistilled
redigatur in pulverem (r. in p. or **red. in pulv.)**: let it be reduced to a powder
redivivus [restored to life]: resuscitated
reductus: reduced
reductus in pulverem (red. in pulv.): reduce to a powder
refrigerans: cooling
regimen: guidance; direction
regio epigastrica: the epigastric region
regio hepatis (reg. hepat.): the region of the liver
regio lumborum: the region of the loins
regio umbilici (reg. umbil.): the umbilical region
regius: royal
reliquum or **reliquus (reli.** or **reliq.)**: the rest; the remaining; the remainder
remedium: remedy; cure

remedium efficacissimum: the most effective cure (i.e., a sovereign remedy)
remisso animo [the inactive mind]: listlessly; listlessness
remissus: relaxed; inactive; also, faint
renes (sing. **ren**): the kidneys
renovetur: let it be renewed
renovo: to renew
repens: sudden; unexpected; also, creeping
repetatur (**rep.** or **repet.** or **rept.**): let it be repeated
res: a thing
residuum: residue
residuus: remaining
resina: resin; rosin
restrictus: confined
rete (pl. **retia**) [a net]: plexus of nerves; vascular network
rete mucosum: the tissue below the skin that gives it its color
reticulatus: netlike
retineatur: let it be retained
retinendus: to be kept or retained
reubarbarum or **rheubarbarum**: rhubarb
rhamnus: buckthorn (properly, **rhamnus cathartica**)
rheumaticus: rheumatic
rhizoma: a rhizome
rhoeas: wild poppy
rhus: sumac
rhus radicans: poison ivy
rhus toxicodendron: poison oak
ribes: currant (see also, **uvae Corinthae**)
ribes aureum: golden currant
ribes grossularia: gooseberry
ribes nigrum: black currant
ribes rubrum or **ribes sanguineum**: red currant
ricinus: the castor plant
rigens: stiff; unbending
rigidus: rigid; stiff; hard
rigor mortis: the stiffening or rigor of the body after death
risus sardonicus: convulsive laughter associated with tetanus
roborans: strengthening
roboratus: strengthened
robustus: robust

rosa: rose; wild rose
rosmarinus: rosemary
rostratus: having a beak
rostrum: beak; snout
rotula: a lozenge
rotundifolius: round-leaved
rubefaciens: blistering; reddened
rubella: the German measles
rubeola: the measles
ruber or **rubrum**: red
rubramentum: red ink
rubus: blackberry
rubus fruticosus: European blackberry
rubus idaeus: raspberry
rubus villosus: blackberry
ructus: belching
rudicula: a spatula; wooden spoon
rudis: a rod
rufus: red; reddish
rugosus: wrinkled
rumex: yellow dock; sorrel (properly, **rumex crispus**)
ruptus: burst open
ruri: in the county
russus: reddish
rutaceus: pertaining to rue

S

sabal: saw palmetto
sabina: savin; red cedar
saccharatus (**sacch.**): sugarcoated
sacchari faex: treacle; molasses
saccharinum: benzosulfinide (i.e., saccharin sweetener)
saccharomyces: yeast
saccharum (**sacch.**): sugar; cane sugar
saccharum fuscum: brown sugar
saccharum lactis: milk sugar; lactose
saccharum purificatum: refined sugar; sucrose
saccus [sack]: a pouch; a filter bag; a pressing cloth for straining wine

sacculus: a small filter; a sack
sacer ignis [sacred fire]: erysipelas
sacer morbis [sacred sickness]: epilepsy
saepe: often
saepius: more often
sal: salt
sal amarus [bitter salt]: a cathartic (e.g., Epsom salt)
sal catharticus: a cathartic (e.g., Epsom salt)
sal culinarius [cooking salt]: table salt
sal gemmae: rock salt
sal prunella: refined potassium nitrate (saltpeter), previously used to alleviate sore throats
sal volatile: aromatic spirit of ammonia (i.e., smelling salts)
saliva: saliva; spittle
salix: willow
saltem: at least; in any event
saluber: healthy; salutary
salubritas: health; soundness; wholesomeness
salus: health; safety; well-being
salutaris: healthful; beneficial
salvia: sage (properly, **salvia officinalis**)
salvo praescripto: except as directed
salvo pudore: without offense to modesty
sambucus: the elder tree (including the flower and berry)
sanctus: sacred; holy; sainted
sanet: let him or her cure
sanguinaria: bloodroot
sanguine suffusus: bloodshot
sanguinis mictus: urine mixed with blood (see also, **mictus cruentus**)
sanguis: blood
sanguisuga: a bloodsucker (i.e., a leech)
sanies: blood-tinged discharge; a discharge from ulcers
sanitas: health; wholeness; sanity
santalinus: of sandalwood
santalum: sandalwood
santonica: wormseed
sanus: sane; healthy
sapo: soap
sapo kalinus: potash soap
saponarius: soapy

saponatus: saponated
sapor: taste; the taste of a thing
saporatus: flavored
sarcophagus: flesh-eating (also, a tomb)
sarza: sarsaparilla
satis: enough
sativus: cultivated
saturatio: saturation
saturatus: full; saturated
scalpellum: a scalpel; a small surgical knife
scalprum: a penknife; a cutting instrument
scammonium: scammony (a gum resin)
scapula (pl. **scapulae**): shoulder blade
scarlatina: scarlet fever
scatula (**scat.**): a box
scatula pilularum: a box of pills
schola medicorum: medical school
scilicet (**sc.** or **scil.**): namely; to wit; that is to say
scilla: squill; sea onion (see also, **urginea**)
scissus: cut; torn; cleft
scoparius: a broom
scorbutus: scurvy
scorpio: a scorpion (see also, **nepa**)
scriptum or **scriptus**: written; scribbled; also, scrawled
scrobiculo cordis (**scrob. cord.**): to the pit of the stomach
scrobiculus cordis: the pit of the stomach
scobis citreus: grated lemon peel
scrofa: a breeding sow (see also, **sus scrofa**)
scrupulus or **scrupulum** (**scr.**): a scruple
scrupulus dimidius: half a scruple
sculpsit (**sc.** or **sculpt.**): he or she carved or engraved it
sculptus: sculpted
scutellaria: skullcap
scutum: a shield
sebum: suet; grease; tallow
sebum bovinum: beef suet
sebum ovillum: mutton suet
secale: rye; ergot
secundis horis (**sec. hor.**): every two hours
secundum (**sec.**): according to

secundum artem (**s.a.** or **S.A.** or **sec. art.**): according to pharmaceutical practice
secundum gustum: according to taste
secundum naturam (**s.n.** or **S.N.** or **sec. nat.**): according to nature; naturally
secundus: the second
sed: but
sedans: a sedative
sedativus: soothing; sedating
sedecim: sixteen
sedes: stool
sedes liquidae: loose stools
sedulo: sedulously; assiduously
selibra: half a pound
semel: once
semel die (**s.d.** or **sem. die**): once a day
semel in die (**s.i.d.** or **S.I.D.** or **sem. in die**): once a day
semen: seed
semicupium: a bath for only part of the body, such as a hip bath
semicyathus: half a glassful
semidrachma (**semidr.**): half a drachm (dram)
semihora (**semih.**): half an hour
seminex: half-dead
seminudus: half-naked
semis ($\bar{s}\,\bar{s}$): half or one half
semivivus: very faint; half-dead
semper: always
sempervirens [always green]: an evergreen
semuncia: half an ounce
senectus: old age
senex: an old man
senilis: aged; senile
senior: older
sensim: gradually; by degrees
sensorium or **sensorium commune**: the seat of sensation; the brain
separatim: separately
sepia: the cuttlefish
septem: seven
septentriones (sing. **septentrio**): the north
septicus: septic

septingenti: seven hundred
septimana: a week
septimus: the seventh
septuaginta: seventy
sepultus (**S.**): buried
septum: a barrier or partition
septum nasi: the division between the nostrils
septum scroti: the partition separating the testicles
sequens: following
sequente luce: the following day
sequestrum: a deposit
sera nocte: late at night
sericum: silk
sericus: silken
seriparus: curdling; curdled
sero: late; at a late hour
serotinus: late-arriving; late-maturing
serpens [creeping animal]: serpent; snake (see also, **anguis**)
serperastra: knee splits or bandages for straightening a crooked leg
serra: a saw
serratifolius: notched-leaved; serrated leaves
serratus: serrated
serrula: a little saw
serrulatus: saw-toothed
serum: serum (i.e., the watery part of blood, curdled milk, *etc.*)
serum lactis: whey
serus: late; too late
sesamum: sesame
sescenti: six hundred
sesqui: one and one half
sesquihora (**sesquih.** or **sesqh.**): an hour and a half
sesuncia (**sesunc.**): an ounce and a half (i.e., one and one half ounces)
seta: a bristle
setosus: bristly
sevum [sebum]: suet
sevum bovinum: beef suet
sevum ovillum: mutton suet
sexaginta: sixty
sexies die (**sex. d.**): six times a day

sexies in die (**sex. in d.**): six times a day
sextarius: a pint
sextis horis (**sext. hor.**): every six hours
sextus: the sixth
sexus: sex (i.e., gender)
sexus muliebris: the female sex
sexus virilis: the male sex
si dolor urgeat (**si dol. urg.**): if the pain is severe
si non valeat (**s.n.v.** or **si non val.**): if it does not respond
si opus sit (**s.o.s.** or **si op. sit**): if necessary; if the occasion requires
si vires permittant (**s.v.p.** or **si vir. perm.**): if strength permits
sic: thus; so
siccant: drying (i.e., a desiccant)
siccat: it dries
siccatus: dried
siccus: dry; desiccated
sidereus: related to the stars; starry
sidus: a star or constellation of stars
signa (**S.** or **Sig.**): write or mark thus on the prescription label
signare: to label
signator (fem. **signatrix**): one who signs or seals a written document
signatura: a signature (see also, **subscriptum**)
signetur (**s.** or **sig.**): let it be written; label it thus
signetur nomine proprio (**s.n.p.** or **sig. nom. prop.**): label with proper name (as opposed to the brand name)
signum: a mark; sign
silvaticus or **sylvaticus**: of the forest; wild
silvestris or **sylvestris**: wooded; wild; growing wild
simia or **simius**: ape; monkey
similis: similar; like
simplex: simple
simul: together; at the same time
simulare morbum: to feign illness
sinapis (**sinap.**): mustard
sinapis nigra: black mustard
sinapismus: a mustard poultice
sinciput: the front of the head (as opposed to **occiput**)
sindon: muslin; fine linen
sine: without
sine aqua: without water; undiluted

sine auxilio: unaided
sine dilatione: without delay
sine dolore: painless
sine igne: without fire (i.e., cold-drawn)
sine maculis [without stain]: spotless
sine mora: without delay
sine sale (**s.s.**): without salt
singillatim: singly; separately; one by one
singula quaque: with each dose
singularis [singular]: each; alone; individual
singuli: singly; each one; one by one
singulis auroris (**sing. auror.**): every morning
singulis horis (**sing. hor.**): every hour
singulorum (**sing.**): of each
singultus: a gasp; a hiccup
singulus (pl. **singuli**): single; separate; apiece
sinister (**sinist.**): left
sinistra: left hand; left side
sipho: a syringe
sipho eburneus: an ivory syringe
sipho vitreus: a glass syringe
sitis: thirst
smilax: greenbrier; sarsaparilla
sol: sun
solanum: nightshade
solaris: solar
solidus: solid
solitus: usual; ordinary
solubilis: soluble
solus: alone
solutio or **solutum** (**sol.**): a solution
solutus: dissolved; loosened
solve (**solv.**): dissolve
solve cum calore (**solv. c̄ cal.**): dissolve by warming
somniferus: sleep inducing
somnium: a dream; also, a daydream
somnolentus: sleepy; drowsy
somnus: sleep
sonitus: a buzzing sound in the ears
sonus: sound

sopiens: sleep-inducing
sopor: deep sleep
soporiferus: inducing deep sleep
sorbilis: drinkable
sorbilo: by sipping; swallowing small drops
sordidus: foul; dirty; vile
soror: sister
spasmus caninus: spasms attending tetanus
spatium: space; interval
spatula or **spathula**: spatula; ladle; a knife for mixing medicines
species: a particular sort, type, or kind
species novum (sp. nov.): a new species
specificum: specific; particular
specillum: a surgeon's probe
specimen: a sample; an example
speculum (pl. **specula**) [a mirror]: a medical instrument used during an examination to dilate or open an orifice or body cavity
spes: hope
sphincter [bracelet]: contracting muscles that surround natural openings
sphincter ani: muscles that close the anus (see also, **constrictor ani**)
sphincter oris: a muscle that closes the mouth
spica (pl. **spicae**): point spike; spur; head of grain
spicatus: spiked
spicula: bone splinter
spiculum (pl. **spicula**): a sharp point; needle; a sting, as by a bee
spina: a spine; a thorn; the backbone
spiracula (sing. **spiriculum**): air holes; spiracles; respiratory pores of the skin
spiritus (s. or **spr.**): a spirit; an alcoholic drink; a spirit of any kind
spiritus chloroformi: chloric ether
spiritus Coloniensis: eau de Cologne (see also, **aqua Coloniensis**)
spiritus frumenti: whiskey
spiritus juniperi: gin
spiritus lenis: smooth breathing; gentle respiration
spiritus myrciae: bay rum
spiritus odoratus: a scented or perfumed spirit (e.g., eau de Cologne)
spiritus sacchari: rum
spiritus tenuior: proof spirit
spiritus vini (s.v. or **spirit. vin.**): wine spirit; an alcoholic spirit

spiritus vini Gallici (**s.v.g.**): brandy (see also, **vini Gallici spiritus**)
spiritus vini methylatus: a methylated spirit
spiritus vini rectificatus (**s.v.r.**): rectified wine spirit; alcohol
spiritus vini tenuis (**s.v.t.**): proof spirit (i.e., a mix of half alcohol and half water)
spiritus vinosus: spirits of wine; alcohol
spissatus: thickened
spissus: thick; solid, not fluid
spleneticus: arising from or affected by the spleen
splenium: an adhesive plaster
spondylus: a vertebra; also, a whirlpool
spongia: sponge
spongiola: a small piece of sponge
sponte: voluntarily; by one's own choice
spumosus: foamy
sputum: spittle
squama [fish scale]: scaly condition of the skin
squamatus: scaly
squamula: a small scale from the skin
squarrosus [scaly]: covered with scales
stadium [race course]: a stage or period; the course of a disease
stagnum [standing water]: a pond or marsh
stanni oxidum: tin oxide powder previously used to make puddy
stannum (**Sn.** or **sn.**): tin
staphisagria: stavesacre
statim (**stat.**): immediately
status: state; condition; also, a standing position or posture
stearicus: stearic (i.e., derived from an animal fat such as tallow)
stella: star
stellans: starry
stent (sing. **stet**): let them stand
stercoreus: filthy
stercus: dung; manure
sterilis: sterile; barren
sterilisatus: sterilized
sterno (**stern.**): to the chest
sternum: chest
sternutatio: sneezing
sternutatorium or **sternutamentum** (**sternut.**): snuff
stertor [snoring]: loud and harsh respiration

stet (**st.**): let it stand
stibium: antimony (see also, **antimonium**)
stigma: a mark on the skin
stillicidium: flowing drop by drop
stillo: to trickle
stilus or **stylus**: a pencil
stimulans: stimulating
stimulus: a stimulant
stomacho jejuno: on a fasting stomach
stomacho vacuo: on an empty stomach
stomachus: the stomach
strabismus: the squinting of one or both eyes
stratum super stratum (**s.s.s.** or **S.S.S.**): layer upon layer
stremma: luxation; a sprain
streptococcicus: streptococcic
stria [furrow]: a mark under the skin that appears in some fevers
striatus: striped
strigosus: thin
struma: swelling; tumor
strychnina: strychnine
stupor: drowsiness; senselessness
stylus or **stilus**: a pencil
stypticus: styptic
sub: under; beneath; up to
sub divo: in the open air
sub finem coctiones: when the boiling is nearly finished
sub verbo (**s.v.**): under the word or heading
sub voce (**s.v.**): under the word or heading
suber: cork; cork tree
suberatus [made of cork]: corked; stoppered
subinde: now and then; repeatedly
subitarius: improvised
subitum: an emergency
subitus: sudden
sublimatus: sublimed
subscriptum [signed]: a signature (see also, **signatura**)
subsultus: twitching
subtepidus: lukewarm
subter: under
subtilis: fine; subtle

subtusus: somewhat bruised
succedaneum: a substitute medicine
succinum or **sucinum**: amber
succirubrus: red-juiced
succus or **sucus**: juice; sap
succus limettae: lime juice
succus limonis: lemon juice
sucidus: juicy; full of sap
sucrosum: sucrose; sugar
sudarium: a towel or handkerchief
sudator (f. **sudatrix**): causing perspiration
sudatorius: a sweating room (e.g., a steam room or sauna)
sudor or **sudatio**: sweat; sweating, perspiration
sudorificus: causing sweat
sufficiens: sufficient
sufflavus: a yellowish color
suffumigatio or **suffitus**: fumigation
suffuscus: darkened; dark brown
suffusus: spread through; steeped; tinged
sugatur (sug.): let it be sucked
suillus: pertaining to swine
sulcus: ditch; trench; the grooves and fissures of the brain
sulfur or **sulphur** (**S.** or **s.**): sulfur; brimstone
sulfurata: brimstone matches
sulfuratus: containing sulfur
sulfuricus: sulfuric
sulfurosus: sulfurous
sumantur (sum.): let them be taken
sumat (sum.): let him or her take
sumat aeger: let the patient take
sumat talem (sum. tal.): take one such
sumatur (sum.): let it be taken
sume (sum.): take
sumendus: to be taken
summa diligentia: with the utmost diligence
summus: the highest; the utmost (as opposed to **infimus** or **infumus**)
super alutam: on leather
super gossypium (sup. gossyp.): upon cotton wool
super linteum (sup. lin.): upon linen
super malas: on the cheeks

supercilium: the eyebrow
superficies: surface; external appearance
superfundo: to pour upon
superior: higher (in position or grade, as opposed to **inferior**)
supernatans: floating on the surface
supersubstantialis: life-sustaining
superus: above; higher (as opposed to **inferus**)
supplementum: supplement
suppositorium (supp. or **suppos.**): a suppository
supra (sup.): above
supra morem: more than usual
supra ulcera: over the sores
suprarenalis: suprarenal (i.e., above the kidney)
sura: the calf of the leg
surculus: a twig
surditas: deafness
surdus: deaf
sus: pig; swine
sus scrofa: hog; swine; a breeding sow (see also, **scrofa**)
suspirium: a deep breath; a sigh
sutura: a suture
suus: his, her, its
sylvaticus or **silvaticus**: of the forest; wild
sylvestris or **silvestris**: growing wild
symptoma: a symptom
synclonus ballismus: the shaking palsy
syncope: a fainting spell
syrupus or **sirupus (syr.**): a syrup
syrupus acaciae: syrup of acacia (used as a demulcent)
syrupus aloe (syr. aloe): aloe syrup
syrupus fuscus (syr. fus.): molasses

T

tabacum: tobacco (see also, **lobelia**)
tabella (tab.): a tablet
taberna: a shop
tabes [wasting away]: decay; consumption of the body
tabidus: melting; dissolving; decaying
tabletta: a small tablet

tabula: a table
taenia: a tapeworm
taenia lata: a species of tapeworm that grows to enormous lengths
taenia saginata: a tapeworm typically found in cows
taenia solium: a tapeworm typically found in pigs
talcum: talc
taleola: a small oblong piece
tales doses (tal. dos.): such doses
talis (tal.): such
talpa: the mole
talus: ankle; ankle bone; also, heel
tamarindus: tamarind
tanacetum: the tansy
tannicus: tannic
tantillum: a little
tantum quantum: just as much as is required
tantus: so much; so great
taraxacum dens-leonis or **taraxacum**: the dandelion (see also, **leontodon taraxacum**)
tardus: slow; late
tarsi oculorum: the eyelids
tarsis oculorum (tars. ocul.): to the eyelids
tarsus: the instep (i.e., the united bones of the foot)
tartaricus: tartaric
taurus: a bull; a steer
taxis [arrangement]: an operation in which an organ is replaced to its natural position by hand
taxus: a yew tree
tectus: covered; concealed
tela: tissue
tela araneae: cobwebs
temperarius: temporary; adapted to time and circumstance
temperatus: tempered; properly mixed
tempora: the temples
tempore (temp.): in the time of
tempus: time; the temple (forehead)
temulentus: intoxicated; tipsy
tenebra: darkness
tenebrosus: dark; gloomy
tendo Achillis or **tendo calcaneus**: the Achilles tendon

tener: tender
tenesmus: a straining during bowel movements but without discharge
tentaculum: a feeler (i.e., an exploratory instrument)
tenuis: thin; slender; weak; diluted
tepefactus: warmed
teridarium: a room containing a warm bath
tepidus: warm or lukewarm
ter [thrice]: three times
ter et quater [three times and four times]: again and again
ter in die (**t.i.d.** or **T.I.D.**): three times a day
ter in hebdomada (**ter in hebdom.** or **t. in hebdom.**): three times a week
ter in hora (**ter in hor.**): three times an hour
ter quaterve die (**t.q.d.**): three or four times a day
ter quotidie (**ter quot.**): three times daily
terantur: let them be rubbed
tere (**ter.**): rub; triturate
tere bene: rub well
tere bene simul (**ter. bene sim.**): rub together well
tere diu: rub for a long time
tere omni: rub all together
tere simul: rub together
terebinthina: turpentine
terebra: a trepan; a gimlet; a borer
terendus: to be rubbed
teres: rounded; polished; well-turned
tergum: the lower back
terra: earth
terra cimolia: fuller's earth
territus: frightened
terror: fear; a fright
tertiis horis (**tert. hor.**): every three hours
tertius: the third
testa: a shell; urn; also, a coating or covering
testa ovi: eggshell
testa praeparata: powdered oyster shell
testis (pl. **testes**): a testicle
tetanicus: related to or characteristic of tetanus, such as neck cramps or spasms
thea: tea

theaepoculum: a teacupful
thebaicus: pertaining to or containing opium
theobroma [food of the gods]: the cacao tree which yields cocoa beans
thermae: warm springs or baths
thermometrum: a thermometer
thoraci (thorac.): to the chest
thoracis: of the chest
thorax: chest; the breastplate
thuja: thuja; arbor vitae or arborvitae tree
thus or **tus**: incense; frankincense
thymus: the thymus gland; also, thyme
thyroideum: the thyroid gland
thyroideus: pertaining to the thyroid
tibia: the shinbone
tiglium: croton (properly, **croton tiglium**)
timidus: timid; fearful
tinctoreus: dyed; colored
tinctura (tinct. or **t.** or **TR)**: tincture; a dye
tinctura ejusdem: tincture of the same (i.e., of the drug immediately preceding)
tincturae: of a tincture
tinea capitis: ringworm of the scalp
tinnitus aurium or **tinnitus**: ringing in the ears
titulus: a label or inscription
toluiferus: producing balsam of tolu
tomentosus: wooly; furry
tonicus: a tonic
tormina: dysentery with gripping pain
torpidus: numb; sluggish
torpor: numbness; lack of sensation
torrefactus: roasted
tostus: toasted; roasted
toties quoties (tot. quot.): as often as; repeatedly; on each occasion
totus: the whole
toxicum: poison
toxitabella: a poison tablet
tractim: in managed bits; by degrees
trans: through; across
trans cribrum: through a sieve
translucidus: translucent; transparent

transversum digitum: a finger's breadth
transversus: transverse
traumaticus: traumatic
trecenti: three hundred
tredecim: thirteen
tremor cordis: palpitation of the heart
tremulus: trembling
tres: three
triandrus: having three stamens
tricupis: three-pointed
triduum (trid.): a period of three days
trifidus: split or divided into three parts; three-pronged or three-forked
trifolium: a clover
trifoliatus: having three leaves
trifolius: three-leaved
trigenta: thirty
trigonalis: three-cornered
trihorium: a period of three hours
trillium: wake robin
tripartitus: three-part
triplex: triple
triplum: three times the amount
trismus: tetanus (i.e., lockjaw)
trismus nascentium: infantile lockjaw
tristis: sad; sorrowful
triticum: wheat (more properly, **triticum aestivum**)
tritu: by rubbing
trituratio: trituration (i.e., reducing something into a powder)
tritus: rubbed; a rubbing; a grinding
trochiscus (troch.): a lozenge
trochlea: a pulley
truncus: stem; trunk
tuber: swelling; protuberance
tubercula (sing. **tuberculum**): small hard tumors
tuberosus: tuberous; lumpy; full of humps or protuberances
tubulatus: formed or shaped like a tube; tubular
tubulus: a small tube
tubus: pipe; tube
tum: at that time
tumidus: swollen

tumor [a swelling]: a protuberance
tunica: a covering
tunicatus (tunicat.): coated
tunicentur cum gelatino (tunic. c̄ gelat.): let them be gelatin coated
tunicentur pilulae (tunic. pil.): let the pills be coated
tunicetur (tunic.): let it be coated
tus or **thus**: incense; frankincense
tussi ingravescente (tuss. ingrav.): with the cough growing worse
tussi molesta (tuss. mol.): with the cough being troublesome
tussi urgente (tuss. urg.): with the cough being severe
tussilago (tussilago farfara): coltsfoot (see also, **farfara**)
tussis (tus.): a cough
tussis convulsiva: whooping cough (see also, **pertussis**)
tussis ferina: a fierce or savage cough
tussis molestante (tuss. mol.): the cough being troublesome
tympanum: the drum of the middle ear
typhosus: pertaining to typhus; typhoid
typhus gravior: a malignant typhus, typically found in military camps (**febris castrensis**) or in prisons (**febris carcerum**)
typus: a mold or pattern (sometimes applied to the form, order, and progress of fevers)
typicus: typical

U

ulcus: sore; ulcer
ulmus: elm
ulmus fulva: slippery elm
ulna: elbow; arm; the lower arm
ultime: finally; at last
ultimo (ult.): the last or previous month
ultimo mense (ult. m.): the last or previous month
ultimo praescriptus (ult. praesc. or **ult. praes.)**: last prescribed; the last ordered
ultimus (ult.): the last
ultra non: no more
umbella: a sunshade
umbelliferus: bearing an umbel
umbilicus: the navel
umbra: shade; shadow

umbrosus: shady
umerus or **humerus**: the shoulder or upper arm
unam ter in die (u.t.i.d.): one three times a day
uncia (oz. or **unc.)**: an ounce
unctio: an anointing
uncus: hook
undecim: eleven
undique: from all sides; everywhere
unguen: a fatty substance; an ointment
unguentatus: anointed
unguentum (ung. or **ungt.)**: an ointment
unguentum aquae rosae: cold cream
unguentum caeruleum: blue mercurial ointment
unguiculus: fingernail or toenail
unguilla: an ointment jar
unguis or **ungula**: nail; claw; hoof; talon
unus: one
urbs: a city or town
urgens: urgent
urginea: squill; sea onion (see also, **scilla**)
urina: urine
urosus: pertaining to urine
ursus (f. **ursa**): a bear
urtica: the nettle
usque (usq.): as far as
usque ad: up to
ustus: burnt
usitatus: used often; commonly used
usus: use
ut: in order that; so that; as
ut ante or **ut antea**: as before
ut assolet: as is customary
ut dictum (ut dict.): as directed
ut heri: as yesterday
ut ne quis utatur: that no one make use of it
utatur: let him or her make use (i.e., benefit)
utendus: to be used
uterque: both of them
uterus: the uterus (i.e., the internal area of the womb)
utilis: useful

utrius libet: of whichever [the patient] pleases
uva: grape
uva ursi: bearberry
uvae Corinthae or **uvae Corinthiacae**: Corinthian grapes or currants (see also, **ribes**)
uvae passae: dried grapes; raisins (see also, **passulae**)
uvula [small grape]: the uvula
uxor (**ux.**): wife

V

vacca: a cow
vaccina or **vaccinia**: cowpox, used as a vaccine against smallpox
vaccinium: a blueberry or cranberry
vaccinum: a vaccine
vaccinum cholerae: cholera vaccine
vaccinum febris flavae: yellow fever vaccine
vaccinum pertussis: whooping cough vaccine
vaccinum rabies: rabies vaccine
vaccinum typhosum: typhoid vaccine
vaccinum variolae: smallpox vaccine
vaccinus: of a cow
vacuo: in a vacuum
vacuum: a vacuum; an empty space
vagina [sheath]: female sex organ
vagina cordis [the case of the heart]: the pericardium
vagitus: a child's cry (i.e., the first cry of a newborn child)
valeriana: valerian
valetudinarius: valetudinarian (i.e., a sick or infirm person)
valetudo: health
valgus: bowlegged (i.e., legs bent outward)
vanilla: vanilla (properly, **vanilla aromatica**)
vanillinum: vanillin
vannus: a winnowing fan
vapor: vapor; steam; an inhalation
varicella: chickenpox
varicosus: having varicose veins
variifolius: having varied leaves
variola: smallpox
variola vaccinae: cowpox

varix: varicose vein
varus: crooked; knock-kneed
varus punctatus: acne
vas (pl. **vasa**) [utensil]: a vessel or duct
vas apertum: an open or uncovered vessel
vas deferens (pl. **vasa deferentia**): the sperm duct
vas fictile: an earthenware vessel
vas vitreum: a glass vessel
vasa vasorum: small blood vessels that supply larger veins
vasa vorticosa: the hairlike veins of the eyes
vasculosus [full of vessels]: vascular
vasculum: a small vessel
vaselinum: petroleum jelly (see also, **petrolatum**)
vasum: a vessel
vegetabilis: (adj.) vegetable
vegetus: fresh; lively; vigorous
vehiculum (vehic.): a vehicle; a means of conveyance
velum: a veil; a screen; a curtain
vena (pl. **venae**): a vein; a blood vessel
vena basilica: the major vein of the arm
vena cava (pl. **venae cavae**): one of the large veins flowing into the heart
venaesectio (vs. or **venaes.**): bleeding; venesection (i.e., bloodletting)
venaesectio brachii: bleeding in the arm
venenosus: poisonous
venenum: venom; poison; drug
venificus: poisonous
venter or **ventriculus**: the belly; the stomach
ventriculo jejuno: on an empty stomach
ver: spring
veratrum: hellebore
verbascum: mullein
verbatim: word for word; literally
verbi gratia (v.g.): for example
verbum (pl. **verba**): word
verbum sapienti (verb. sap.): a word to the wise
vermiculatus: to be full of worms
vermiculus: a worm
vermifuges: a vermifuge
vermis (pl. **vermes**): a worm

vernalis: pertaining to spring
vernix: a varnish
vernus: of spring; vernal
verruca: a wart
versicolor: variegated; changing color
versus (**v.** or **vs.**): against
vertebra (pl. **vertebrae**): a vertebra (i.e., one of the twenty-four bones of the spinal column)
vertex: the crown of the head
vertigo [whirling round]: dizziness; lightheadedness
verum: truth
verus: true; genuine
vesania: madness; insanity
vesica: the bladder
vesicalis: pertaining to the bladder
vesicans: blistering
vesicatorius: pertaining to a blister
vesiculosus: full of blisters
vespa: a wasp
vesper (**vesp.**): evening
vesperi (**vesp.**): in or of the evening
vespertinus: in the evening
vestimentum [vestment]: clothing; bed clothes
veterinarius: veterinary; veterinarian
veterinus: a beast of burden
vetus: old
via: way
viae lachrymalis: the tear ducts
vibix (pl. **vibices**): a mark from a blow; a weal or welt
vice versa (**v.v.**): conversely
vices (**vic.**): time; times; turn
vicesimus: twentieth
vicissim: alternately
victus: nourishment
vide infra (**v.i.**): see below
vide supra (**v.s.**): see above
videlicet (**viz.**): namely; to wit
vigilia: sleeplessness
viginti: twenty
viginti et quattuor: twenty-four

villosus: hairy; shaggy
vina medicata: medicated wines
vincit: it conquers
vini Gallici spiritus: brandy (see also, **spiritus vini Gallici**)
vinosus: vinous; containing or pertaining to wine
vinum (vin.): wine
vinum album: white wine (see also, **vinum xericum**)
vinum antimonii: wine of antimony (see also, **antimonii vinum**)
vinum opii: wine of opium
vinum portense or **portensis**: port wine
vinum rubrum: red wine
vinum stibiatum: antimonial wine
vinum xericum: sherry (see also, **xericus**)
vinylicus: vinyl
viola: violet
violaceus: violet (color)
vipera: viper
vir: man
vires: strength
vires corporis: bodily strength
virga: a rod
virga vitrea: a glass rod
virginale claustrum: the hymen
viridis (vir. or **virid.)**: green
virosus: fetid; poisonous
virus: poison; a poison fluid
vis (pl. **vires**): strength; power; force
vis a tergo: a force or power from behind
vis formativa: the body's own power to grow and nourish itself
vis inertiae: force of inertia
vis medicatrix: healing power
vis vitae (or **vis vitalis**): vital power; life force
viscera (sing. **viscus**): internal organs (i.e., the guts)
viscidus: sticky
viscus quercus or **viscum album**: mistletoe
vita: life
vita propria: the vital power peculiar to any organ
vitello ovi solutus (v.o.s.): dissolve in egg yolk
vitellus ovi or **vitellus**: an egg yolk (see also, **ovi vitellus**)
vitis: grapevine

vitreus: of glass
vitrum: glass
vitulus: a calf
vividus: lively; animated
vivus: living
vix: with effort; with difficulty; scarcely
vixit . . . annos (v.a.): he or she lived . . . years
volatilis: volatile
volvendus (volvend.): to be rolled
vomica: an ulcer or sore; a boil
vomicus: an emetic; having emetic properties
vomitio (vomit.): the act of vomiting
vomitione urgente (vom. urg.): the vomiting becoming serious
vomitorius: an emetic to elicit vomiting
vomitu finito (vom. fin.): the vomiting having ceased
vomitus: vomit
vomitus cruentus: bloody vomit (i.e., hematemesis)
vorax: voracious
vox (pl. **voces**): voice
vox abscissa: loss of voice
vox capitis: a falsetto voice
vulgaris: common
vulgo: commonly
vulnus: an injury; a wound
vulpis morbus: alopecia (see also, **morbus vulpis**)
vulpes: a fox
vultus: the face; countenance
vulva: the vulva (i.e., the external area of the womb)

X

xanthoxylum: prickly ash
xericus (xer.): sherry (see also, **vinum xericum**)
xiphias: swordfish (properly, **xiphias gladius**)

Z

zea: corn silk
zea mays: maize; Indian corn (see also, **mays**)
zebratus: zebra-striped; striped across

zephyrus: a warm west wind
zotheca: a private room
zincum (**Zn.**): zinc
zingiber (**zz.**): ginger
ziziphus: the jujube tree or its fruit
zona: a girdle, applied to the shingles
zygoma: the cheekbone (see also, **os jugale** or **os malare**)
zymosis: leavening; fermentation

Selected Maxims and Quotations

On Life, Death, Sickness, and the Healing Arts

Accipe nunc, victus tenuis quid quantaque secum afferat. In primis valeas bene: Now learn what and how great a benefit moderate diet brings with it. Before all, you will enjoy good health (Horace).

Ad extremos morbos, extrema remedia exquisite optima: The greater the sickness, the more vigorous the remedy (Hippocrates).

Adeo in teneris consuescere multum est: So much depends upon habit in the tender years (Virgil).

Aegrescit(que) medendo: The patient grows worse with the treatment (i.e., the remedy is worse than the disease) (Virgil).

Aegri quia non omnes convalescunt, idcirco ars nulla medicina est: Because all the sick do not recover, therefore medicine is not an art (Cicero).

Aegri somnia vana: The delusive dreams of the sick (i.e., hallucinations or nightmares) (Horace).

Aegroto dum anima est, spes est: To the sick, while there is life there is hope (Cicero).

Alia tendanda via est: Another way must be tried (Virgil).

Alter alteris auxilio eget: One requires the aid of the other (Sallust).

Anceps remedium (est) melius quam nullum: A doubtful remedy is better than none (attributed to Sir Percival Pott).

Animal implume bipes: A two-legged featherless animal (definition of man, as attributed to Plato).

Apio opus est: There is need of parsley (a maxim indicating that there is no hope of recovery as parsley was traditionally strewn over graves).

Aurea mediocritas: The golden mean (i.e., moderation in all things) (Horace).

Aut inveniam viam aut faciam: Either I will find a way or I will make one (attributed to Hannibal).

Bibamus, moriendum est: Let us drink, death is certain (Seneca the Elder).

Contra malum mortis, non est medicamen in hortis: Against the evil of death there is no remedy in the gardens (a variation on the previous entry) (a Latin maxim).

DOI: 10.4324/9781003255352-2

Contra vim mortis non crescit herba in hortis: No herb grows in the gardens against the power of death (i.e., there is no remedy against the power of death) (a Latin maxim).

Contraria contrariis curantur: Opposite cures opposite (a principle of homeopathy).

Corpora lente augescunt cito extinguuntur: Bodies are slow in growth, rapid in decay (Horace).

Corpore sed mens est aegro magis aegra; malique in circumspectu stat sine fine sui: The mind is sicker than the sick body; in contemplation of its sufferings it becomes hopeless (Ovid).

Corporis et fortunae bonorum, ut initium, finis est. Omnia orta occidunt, et aucta senescunt: The blessings of good health and good fortune, as they have a beginning, must also have an end. Everything rises but to fall, and grows but to decay (Sallust).

Corpus non animae domicilium sed diversum est: The body is not the abode of the soul but its enemy (Willett's *Emblem Book*, no. 87, after St. Paul).

Crede mihi, miseris coelestia numina parcunt; nec semper laesos, et sine fine, premunt: Believe me, the gods spare the afflicted, and do not always oppress those who are unfortunate (Ovid).

Crescit indulgens sibi dirus hydrops: The fatal dropsy gains on the patient from gratifying his own thirst (Horace).

Crudelem medicum intemperans aeger facit: A disorderly patient makes the physician cruel (Publilius Syrus).

Cuncta prius tentata; sed immedicabile vulnus. Ense recidendum, ne pars sincera trahatur: Every remedy was first tried; but a wound that responds to no cure must be cut away lest the sound part should be affected (Ovid).

Deus est mortali iuvare mortalem: For mortal to help mortal—this is God (Pliny the Elder).

Doctrina est ingenii naturale quoddam pabulum: Learning is a kind of natural food for the mind (Cicero).

Durate et vosmet rebus servate secundis: Carry on and preserve yourselves for better times (Virgil).

Eripit interdum, modo dat medicina salutem: Medicine sometimes snatches away health, sometimes restores it (Ovid).

Errare humanum est: To err is human (Pope, after St. Jerome).

Exigua pars est vitae quam nos vivimus: The part of life which we really live is short (Seneca).

Extrema primo nemo tentavit loco: No one tries extreme remedies at first (Seneca).

Facile omnes cum valemus recta consilia aegrotis damus. Tu si hic sis aliter senties: It is easy for us to give the right advice to the sick when we all are well. Were you in my place, you would feel otherwise (Terence).

Famem vini potio solvit: A drink of wine relieves hunger (Hippocrates).

Felix qui potuit rerum cognoscere causas: Happy is the one who knows (or understands) the causes of all things (Virgil).

Festinat enim decurrere velox flosculus angustae miseraeque brevissima vitae portico; dum bibimus dum sera unguenta puellas poscimus obrepit non intellecta senectus: The short bloom of our brief and narrow life flies fast away; while we are calling for flowers and wine and women, old age is upon us (Juvenal).

Fiat experimentum in corpore vili: Let the experiment be done upon a worthless body (or object) (adapted from Plato).

Fingunt se medicos quivis idiota: Any idiot is ready to prescribe for you in sickness (a medieval proverb).

Fit erranti medicina confessio: Confession is as healing medicine to one who has erred (Cicero).

Graviora quaedam sunt remedia periculis: Some remedies are worse than the disease itself (Publilius Syrus).

Habenda ratio valetudinis: Taking measured account of our health (Cicero).

Hominem non morbum cura: Treat the person, not the disease (motto of the Far Eastern University).

Injuriarum remedium est oblivio: The remedy for wrongs is to forget them (Publilius Syrus).

Male secum agit aeger, medicum qui heredem facit: The sick man does injustice to himself who makes his physician his heir (Publilius Syrus).

Maximum remedium est irae mora: Delay is the greatest remedy for anger (Seneca).

Medice, cura te ipsum: Physician, heal thyself (quoted in St. Luke 4:23).

Medici, causa morbi inventa, curationem inventam putant: Physicians, having discovered the cause of the disease, believe that they have also found the cure (Cicero).

Medici graviores morbos asperis remediis curant: Physicians cure grave diseases with sharp remedies (Curtius).

Medicina mortuorum sera est: Medicine is too late for the dead (Quintilian).

Medicus curat, natura sanat: A doctor treats, nature heals (a proverb).

Medicus dedit qui temporis morbo curam, is plus remedii quam cutis sector dedit: The physician who gives the disease time for cure finds a better remedy than the one who cuts the skin (Erasmus, after Euripides).

Medicus enim nihil aliud est quam animi consolatio: A doctor is nothing if not a consolation to the spirit (also rendered, A doctor is nothing but a sop to conscience) (Petronius).

Mens agitat molem: Mind moves the mass (i.e., Mind moves matter) (Virgil).

Mens sana in corpore sano: A sound mind in a sound body (shortened version of Juvenal).

Mille mali species, mille salutis erunt: There are a thousand forms of evil; there will be a thousand remedies (Ovid).

Mors laborum ac miseriarum quies est: Death is repose from all our toils and miseries (Cicero).

Mors sola fatetur quantula sint hominum corpuscula: Death alone reveals how small men's bodies are (Juvenal).

Mortem misericors saepe pro vita dabit: Mercy often means giving death, not life (Seneca).

Multas cautiones habet: One must take many precautions (a proverb, after Cicero).

Multitudo (autem) sapientium sanitas orbis terrarum: A multitude of the wise is the health of the world (Holbein, after Wisdom of Solomon 6:26).

Nauseanti stomacho effluunt omnia: Everything is thrown off from a sick stomach (anonymous saying).

Nec mihi mors gravis est posituro morte dolores: Death is not grievous to me, for I shall lay aside my pains by death (Ovid).

Nemo quam bene vivat, sed quamdiu, curat; quum omnibus possit contingere ut bene vivat, ut diu nulli: No one cares how well they live, but only how long; it is within the reach of every one to live well, it is within no one's power to live long (Seneca).

Nihil differt utrum aegrum in ligneo lecto an in aureo colloces; quocumque illum transtuleris, morbum suum secum transfert: It matters not whether you place the sick on a bed of wood or gold; wherever you take him his disease comes along (Seneca).

Nisi carenti doloribus morbisque vita ipsa poene fit: For those without care from pain, life itself becomes punishment (Pliny the Elder).

Non ignara mali, miseris succerrere disco: Not unacquainted with misfortune, I learn to give aid to those in misery (Virgil).

Non omnibus aegris eadem auxilia conveniunt: The same remedies do not suit every patient (Celsus).

Nosce tempus: Know your time (an adage, after Erasmus).

Omne vivum ex ovo: Everything living comes from an egg (attributed to William Harvey).

Omnes humanos sanat medicina dolores; solus amor morbi non amat artificem: Medicine cures all human pains; only love-sickness refuses a physician (Sextus Propertius).

Omnia bona bonis: All things are good to the good (a heraldry motto, after St. Paul).

Omnia orta occident: All things that rise also set (Sallust).

Optanda mors ets, sine metu mortis mori: To die without fear of death is to be desired (Seneca).

Orandum est ut sit mens sana in corpore sano: You should pray to have a sound mind in a sound body (Juvenal).

Ornat spina rosas, mella tegunt apes: The rose is guarded by thorns, and honey is protected by bees (Ovid).

Pars sanitatis velle sanari fuit: It is part of the cure to wish to be cured (Seneca).

Pharmaca das aegroto, aurum tibi porrigit aeger, tu morbum curas illius, ille tuum: You give medicine to a sick man, he hands you gold; you cure his sickness and he cures yours (Martius).

Post prandium stabis, post coenam ambulabis: After dinner take rest, after supper take a walk (Scuola Medica Salernitana).

Post tenebras lux: After darkness light (after Job 17:12 in the Vulgate).

Posteri dies testes sunt sapientissimi: Succeeding days are the wisest evidences (a proverb).

Prima quae vitam dedit hora, carpit: The hour which gives us life begins to take it away (Seneca).

Primum non nocere: First to do no harm (attributed to Hippocrates).

Principiis obsta; sero medicina paratur cum mala per longas convaluere moras: Stop it at the beginning; it is too late for medicine to be prepared when disease has grown strong through long delays (Ovid).

Pulvis et umbra sumus: We are dust and shadows (Horace).

Quae prosunt omnibus artes: The arts which are of service to all (i.e., medicine) (Ovid).

Qui nunc it per iter tenebricosum illuc, unde negant redire quemquam: Who now goes through the shadowy path, from whence they say no one returns (Catullus).

Quod nullis amor est medicabilis herbis: Love cannot be cured by herbs (Ovid).

Semita certe tranquillae per virtutem patet unica vitae: The only path to a tranquil life is through virtue (Juvenal).

Senectus ipsa morbus est: Old age is itself a sickness (Terence).

Si ventri bene, si lateri pedibusque tuis, nil divitiae poterunt regales addere majus: If it is well with your stomach, your lungs, and your feet, the wealth of kings cannot add more (Horace).

Sic habeto, non esse te mortalem, sed corpus hoc: Be sure that it is not you that is mortal but only your body (Cicero).

Similia similibus curantur: Like cures like (a principle of homeopathy).

Sine remediis medicina debilis est: Without remedies medicine is powerless (anonymous saying).

Spiritus intus alit; totamque infusa per artus mens agitat molem et magno se corpore miscet: The spirit within nourishes; in all the limbs mind moves the mass and mingles with the mighty frame (Virgil).

Stans pede in uno: Standing on one foot (i.e., done without effort) (Horace).

Stultorum incurata malus pudor ulcera celat: It is the false shame of fools to hide their uncured wounds (Horace).

Summum bonum appertere est bene vivere: To seek the highest good is to live well (St. Augustine).

Summum bonum medicinae sanitas: The highest good of medicine is health (Marlowe).

Tacitum vivit sub pectore vulnus: The unuttered wound lies deep within the breast (Virgil).

Temporis ars medicina fere est: Time is generally the best medicine (Ovid).

Tempus molestiis medetur omnibus: Time heals all wounds (figuratively, after Euripides).

Timidi est optare necem: To wish for death is a coward's part (Ovid).

Totus in toto, et totus in qualibet parte: Wholly complete, and complete in every part (i.e., the human heart) (after St. Thomas Aquinas).

Turpe est doctoris cum culpa redarguit ipsum: It is improper for a doctor to indulge in what he forbids others (Cato).

Ubi desinit philosophus, ibi incipit medicus: Where the philosopher ends, the physician begins (Marlowe).

Varia vita est: Life is changeable (Plautus).

Velut aegri somnia, vanae finguntur species: Just as a sick man's dreams, creating empty fancies (Horace).

Venienti occurrite morbo: Confront the coming disease (i.e., prevention is better than cure) (Persius).

Vis medicatrix naturae: The healing power of nature (attributed to Hippocrates).

Vita brevis, ars longa, occasio praeceps, experientia fallax, judicium difficile: Life is short, art long; occasion fleeting; experience deceiving; judgment difficult (Hippocrates).

Abbreviations

A

a.c. [ante cibos]: before meals
a.c. [ante cibum]: before food
A.D. [anno Domini]: in the year of our Lord
a.d.a. [ante dispensationem agita]: shake before dispensing
a.h.l. [ad hunc locum]: at this place
a.h.v. [ad hanc vocem]: at this word
a.j. [ante jentaculum]: before breakfast
a.m. or **A.M.** [ante meridiem or ante meridianus]: before noon
a.m. or **A.M.** [ante mortem]: before death
a.v. [ad valorem]: according to the value
a.v. [annos vixit]: he or she lived (so many years)
aa or **āā** [ana]: of each
ab init. [ab initio]: from the beginning
abs. febr. [absente febre]: in the absence of fever
acerb. [acerbus]: sour; bitter
acet. [acetum]: vinegar
ad 2 vic. [ad duas vices]: in two doses
ad 2nd vic. [ad secundum vicem]: at twice taking; for the second time
ad 3 al. vic. [ad tres alias vices]: at or for three other times
ad 3 vic. [ad tres vices]: at or for three times
ad alv. excitand. [ad alvum excitatandum]: to stimulate the bowels
ad apt. crass. [ad aptam crassitudinem]: to a suitable consistency
ad def. animi [ad defectionem animi]: to fainting
ad duas vic. [ad duas vices]: in two doses
ad inf. or **ad infin.** [ad infinitum]: to infinity (i.e., forever)
ad init. [ad initium]: at the beginning
ad int. [ad interim]: in the meantime; meanwhile; temporarily
ad lib. [ad libitum]: at will
ad loc. [ad locum]: to or at the place
ad part. dol. [ad partes dolentes]: to the painful parts
ad recid. praec. [ad recidivum praecavendum]: to prevent a relapse
ad sat. [ad saturandum]: to saturation
ad sec. vic. [ad secundum vicem]: for the second time

DOI: 10.4324/9781003255352-3

ad ter. vic. [ad tertiam vicem]: for the third time
ad us. [ad usum]: according to usage
ad us. ext. [ad usum externum]: for external use
ad val. [ad valorem]: according to value
add. or **ad.** [adde]: let there be added
addend. [addendus]: to be added
adhib. or **adhibend.** [adhibendus]: to be used; to be applied
adi. or **adj.** [adiectivum]: adjective
admov. [admove]: apply
admov. [admoveatur]: let it be applied
adst. febr. [adstante febre]: in the presence of fever
adv. [adversum or adversus]: against
aeg. [aeger]: the patient
aeq. [aequalis]: equal
Ag. or **ag.** [argentum]: silver
aggred. febr. [aggrediente febre]: on the approach of fever
agit. [agita]: shake
agit. vas. [agitato vase]: the vial being shaken
alb. [albus]: white
alt. . . . alt. . . . [alter . . . alter . . .]: the one . . . and the other . . .
alt. anni. [alternis annis]: every other year
alt. die. [alternis diebus]: every other day
alt. hor. [alternis horis]: every other hour
alv. adst. [alvo adstricta]: the bowels being constricted (i.e., con-stipated)
alv. laxat. [alvo laxata]: the bowels being relaxed
amp. [amplus]: large; ample
ant. cen. [ante cenam]: before supper
ant. cib. [ante cibos]: before meals
ant. cib. [ante cibum]: before food
ant. coen. [ante coenam]: before supper
ant. disp. agit. [ante dispensationem agita]: shake before dispensing
ant. jentac. [ante jentaculum]: before breakfast
ant. prand. [ante prandium]: before dinner
aper. [aperiens]: opening; aperient (e.g., a laxative)
applicet. [applicetur]: let it be applied
aq. [aqua]: water
aq. aerat. [aqua aerata]: carbonated water
aq. astr. [aqua astricta]: ice
aq. bull. [aqua bulliens]: boiling water
aq. calid. [aqua calida]: warm water

aq. comm. [aqua communis]: tap water
aq. dest. [aqua destillata]: distilled water
aq. dul. [aqua dulcis]: fresh water
aq. ferv. [aqua fervens]: hot water
aq. fluv. [aqua fluvialis]: river water
aq. font. [aqua fontalis or aqua fontana or aqua fontis]: spring water
aq. fort. [aqua fortis]: nitric acid
aq. gel. [aqua gelida]: cold water
aq. mar. [aqua marina]: seawater
aq. naph. [aqua naphae]: orange-flower water
aq. niv. [aqua nivalis]: snow water
aq. pluv. [aqua pluvialis or aqua pluvia]: rainwater
aq. pur. [aqua pura]: distilled water
aq. reg. [aqua regia]: royal water (a mixture that dissolves platinum and gold)
aq. ros. [aqua rosae]: rose water
aq. sal. [aqua saliens]: a jet of water
aq. sals. [aqua salsa]: salty water; salt water
aq. vit. [aqua vitae]: a distilled spirit
arom. [aromaticus]: aromatic
Au. or **au.** [aurum]: gold
aug. [augeatur]: let it be increased
aur. [auri; pl. auribus]: to or for the ear(s)
aur. dext. [auris dextra]: the right ear
aur. laev. [auris laeva]: the left ear
aurin. [aurinarium]: an ear cone; an ear suppository
auristill. [auristillae]: ear drops
austr. [australis]: southern

B

b. [beatus]: blessed; deceased
B.A. [balneum arenae]: a sand bath
b.i.d. [bis in die]: twice a day
B.M. [balneum maris]: a saltwater bath
B.M. [beatae memoriae]: of blessed memory
b.p. [bonum publicum]: the common good
b.t.d. [bis terve die]: two or three times a day
b.t.i.d. [bis terve in die]: two or three times a day
B.V. [balneum vaporis]: a vapor or steam bath

b.v. [bene vale]: farewell
Ba. [barium]: barium
baln. [balneum or balineum]: bath; bathing room
baln. anima. [balneum animale]: part of a freshly killed animal applied to a patient's body or limb
baln. aren. [balneum arenae]: a sand bath
baln. mar. [balneum maris]: a saltwater bath
baln. med. [balneum medicatum]: a medicated bath
baln. sicc. [balneum siccum]: a bath of dry ashes
baln. vap. [balneum vaporis]: a vapor or steam bath
balsam. [balsamum]: balsam
bib. [bibe]: drink
bol. [bolus]: a large pill
bor. [borealis]: northern
brach. [brachio]: the upper arm; to the arm
brom. [bromidum]: bromide
buginar. [buginarium]: a nasal bougie
bull. [bulliat]: let it boil
but. [butyrum]: butter

C

c̄ [cum]: with
c̄ **aq.** [cum aqua]: with water
c̄ **c.** [cum cibos]: with meals
c̄ **c.** [cum cibum]: with food
c̄ **dup.** [cum duplo]: with twice as much
c̄ **pt. aeq.** [cum parte aequale]: with an equal quantity
c̄ **pen.** [cum penicillo]: with a camel-hair brush
c̄ **sem.** [cum semisse]: with an added half
c̄ **tant.** [cum tanto]: with as much
C or **C.** [congius]: a gallon
c. or **ca.** [circa]: about; near; around
c. or **circ.** [circiter]: about
c. or **circ.** [circum]: around; about
c.c. [cornu cervi]: hartshorn
c.c.u. [cornu cervi ustum]: burnt hartshorn
c.m. [cras mane]: tomorrow morning (i.e., the next morning)
c.m.s. [cras mane sumendus]: to be taken tomorrow morning (i.e., the next morning)

c.n. [cras nocte]: tomorrow night
c.n.s. [cras nocte sumendus]: to be taken tomorrow night (i.e., the next evening)
c.v. [cras vespere]: tomorrow evening
c.v. [curriculum vitae]: a résumé
caerul. [caeruleus]: blue
cal. [calefactus]: warmed
calom. [calomelas]: calomel
Cantab. [Cantabrigiensis]: of Cambridge
cap. [cape]: take
cap. [capiant]: let them take
cap. [capiat]: let him or her take
cap. [capiti]: to the head
cap. [capsula]: capsule
capiend. [capiendus]: to be taken
caps. [capsula]: capsule
caps. amylac. [capsula amylacea]: a cachet; a konseal wafer
caps. gelat. [capsula gelatina]: a gelatin capsule
caps. vitrea [capsula vitrea]: a glass capsule
carbas. [carbasus]: gauze
cat. or **catap.** or **cataplasm.** [cataplasma]: a poultice
cent. [centum]: one hundred
cerat. [ceratum]: cerate
cereol. [cereolus]: an urethral bougie
cet. par. [ceteris paribus]: other things being equal
cf. [confer]: compare
chart. [charta]: paper; powder [wrapped in paper]
chart. cerat. [charta cerata]: waxed paper
chartul. [chartula]: small paper; small powder [wrapped in paper]
cib. [cibus]: food; a meal
cito disp. [cito dispensatur]: let it be dispensed quickly
cl. [chlorum]: chlorine
coch. [cochleare or cocleare]: spoon; a spoonful
coch. amp. or **coch. ampl.** [cochleare amplum]: a dessertspoonful
coch. infant. [cochleare infantis]: a teaspoonful
coch. mag. [cochleare magnum]: a tablespoonful
coch. mag. ij [cochlearia magna duo]: two tablespoonfuls
coch. mag. mens. [cochleare magnum mensura]: a measured tablespoonful
coch. max. [cochleare maximum]: a tablespoonful

coch. med. [cochleare medium]: a dessertspoonful
coch. medio. [cochleare mediocre]: a dessertspoonful
coch. min. [cochleare minimum]: a teaspoonful
coch. mod. [cochleare modicum]: a dessertspoonful
coch. parv. [cochleare parvum]: a teaspoonful
coch. parv. iij [cochlearia parva tria]: three teaspoonfuls
coch. plen. [cochleare plenum]: a tablespoonful
colat. [colatus]: strained
colen. [colentur]: let them be strained
colet. [coleatur]: let it be strained
coll. [collyrium]: an eyewash
collod. [collodium]: a collodion
collun. [collunarium]: a nasal douche
collut. [collutorium]: a mouthwash
collyr. [collyrium]: an eyewash
comp. [compositus]: compound
con. [conjunx or coniunx]: wife; spouse
con. [contra]: against
conf. [confectio or confectum]: a confection
cong. [congius]: a gallon
conj. [conjunx or coniunx]: wife; spouse
cons. [conserva]: a conserve; a preserve (i.e., a jam or confection)
consperg. [consperge]: sprinkle; dust
cont. [contusus]: crushed; bruised
cont. bon. mor. [contra bonos mores]: contrary to good manners (or morals)
cont. rem. [continuantur remedia]: let the remedy be continued
contin. [continuetur]: let it be continued
coq. [coque or coquatur]: boil or let it be boiled
coq. ad med. consump. [coque ad medietatis consumptionem]: boil to the consumption of half (i.e., render by one-half)
coq. in S.Q.A. [coque in sufficiente quantitate aquae]: boil in a sufficient quantity of water
coq. S.A. [coque secundum artem]: boil according to practice (i.e., approved pharmaceutical method)
corp. [corpori]: to the body
cort. [cortex]: a peel; rind; outer layer (e.g., bark)
cotid. [cotidianus or cotidie]: daily
crast. [crastinus]: of tomorrow; on the morrow
crep. [crepitus]: discharge of wind or gas from the bowels

crepus. [crepusculum]: twilight; in the evening
cu. [cuprum]: copper
cuj. lib. [cujus libet]: of whatever pleases
curat. [curatio]: a dressing
cyath. amp. [cyathus amplus]: a tumblerful
cyath. mag. [cyathus magnus]: a tumblerful
cyath. med. [cyathus medius]: a small tumbler or claret glassful
cyath. mod. [cyathus modicus]: a small tumbler or claret glassful
cyath. parv. [cyathus parvus]: a wineglassful
cyath. vin. [cyathus vinosis]: a wineglassful
cyath. vinar. [cyathus vinarius]: a wineglassful

D

d. [da]: give
d. [dentur]: let them be given
d. [detur]: let it be given
d. ex d. [diem ex die]: from day to day
d. in p. aeq. [dividatur in partes aequales]: let it be divided into equal parts
D.Ch. [Doctor Chirurgiae]: Doctor of Surgery
d.d. [dono dedit]: given as a gift
d.p. or **D.P.** [directione propria]: with proper directions
d.s.p. [decessit sine prole]: died without issue
D.T. [delirium tremens]: trembling delirium caused by alcohol poisoning
d.t.d. iv [dentur tales doses iv]: let four such doses be given
d.t.d. or **D.T.D.** [detur talis dosis]: give of such a dose
D.V. or **d.v.** [Deo Volente]: God willing
dand. [dandus]: to be given
de d. in d. [de die in diem]: from day to day
deaur. pil. [deaurentur pilulae]: let the pills be gilded (i.e., coated)
deb. spiss. [debita spissitudine]: of a proper thickness or consistency
dec. [decanta]: pour off
decimil. [decimillilitra]: a decimilliliter
decoct. [decoctio or decoctum]: a decoction
decub. [decubitus]: lying down; having gone to bed
decub. hor. [decubitus hora]: at bedtime
deglut. [deglutiatur]: let it be swallowed
dej. alv. [dejectiones alvi]: evacuation of the bowels (i.e., stools)
del. [delineavit]: he or she drew it

depilat. [depilatorium]: a depilatory
dg. or **dgrm.** [decigramma]: a decigram
dieb. alt. [diebus alternis]: every other day
dieb. tert. [diebus tertiis]: every third day
dil. [dilue]: dilute or dissolve
dil. [dilutus]: diluted
diluc. [diluculum]: the break of day; in the morning
dilut. [dilutus]: diluted
dim. [dimidius]: one-half
dimid. [dimidium]: half; the half
direc. prop. [directione propria]: with proper directions
disp. [dispensa]: dispense
div. [dividatur]: let it be divided
div. [divide]: divide
div. in par. aeq. [dividatur in partes aequales]: let it be divided into equal parts
dol. urg. [dolore urgente]: with the onset of pain; when the pain is severe
dolent. part. [dolenti parti]: to the painful part
dolent. part. [dolentibus partibus]: to the painful parts
don. [donec]: until
dos. [dosis]: dose
dos. aug. ad gtt. ij [dosis augeatur ad guttas ij]: let the dose be increased to two drops
dos. aug. ad gtt. iij [dosis augeatur ad guttas iij]: let the dose be increased to three drops
dos. aug. ad gtt. iv [dosis augeatur ad guttas iv]: let the dose be increased to four drops
dr. [drachma]: a drachm (dram)
dram. [drachma]: a drachm (dram)
dup. [duplum]: twice as much
dur. dolor. [durante dolore]: during the pain; the pain continuing
dur. feb. [durante febre]: during the fever; the fever continuing

E

e lact. [e lacte]: with milk
e paul. aq. [e paullo aquae]: with a little water
e paux. aq. [e pauxillo aquae]: with very little water
e quol. veh. [e quolibet vehiculo]: with any vehicle

e quov. liq. [e quovis liquido]: with any liquid
e vehic. crass. [e vehiculo crasso]: in a thick vehicle
e vin. [e vino]: with wine
e.g. [exempli gratia]: for example
e.m.p. [ex modo praescripto]: after the manner prescribed
e.o. [ex officio]: by virtue of office
ead. [eadem]: the same
eburn. [eburneus]: made of ivory
ed. [edulcora]: sweeten; to make more palatable
ed. [edulcoratus]: sweetened; made palatable
ejusd. [ejusdem]: of the same
elix. [elixir] (a magical potion): a medicinal liquid, such as cough medicine
emp. [emplastrum]: a plaster
en. or **enem.** [enema]: an enema; a clyster
esur. [esuriens]: fasting
et al. [et alia]: and other things
et al. [et alibi]: and elsewhere
et al. [et alii or et aliae]: and others
et conj. [et conjunx]: and spouse
et seq. [et sequens]: and the following
et seqq. [et sequentes or et sequentia]: and what follows
et ux. [et uxor]: and wife
etc. [et cetera]: and the rest; and so on
evan. [evanesco or evanescere]: to disappear; vanish; weaken
ex aq. [ex aqua]: in water
ex. gr. [exempli gratia]: for example
exc. [excudit]: he or she fashioned it
exhib. [exhibeatur]: let it be exhibited or given
ext. [extende]: spread; apply
ext. [extractum]: an extract
ext. sup. alut. [extende super alutam]: spread upon leather
extr. [extractum]: an extract

F

F. or **f.** [fac]: make
f. [femina]: female; a woman
f. [fiat or fiant]: let it be made; let them be made
f. [folio]: page

f.l.a. or **F.L.A.** [fiat lege artis]: let it be made according to practice
f.r. [folio recto]: on the front of the page (i.e., the right-hand page)
f.s.a.r. or **F.S.A.R.** [fiat secundum artis regulas]: let it be made according to the rules of practice
f.v. [folio verso]: on the back of the page (i.e., the left-hand page)
far. [farina]: flour; meal
Fe. [ferrum]: iron
feb. dur. [febre durante]: during the fever; the fever continuing
fec. [fecit]: he or she made or did it
ferr. [ferrum]: iron
ferv. [fervens]: hot; boiling
ff. [fecerunt]: they made or did it
ff. [folia]: pages
fi. fa. [fieri facias]: cause it to be done
fict. [fictilis]: made of clay
fl. [flores]: flowers
fl. or **fld.** [fluidus]: fluid; liquid
fl. or **flor.** [floruit]: flourished
flav. [flavus]: yellow
fldext. or **fldxt.** [fluidextractum]: fluidextract
fol. [folium]: a leaf
fort. [fortis]: strong
fract. dos. [fracta dosi]: broken into doses; in divided doses
freq. [frequenter]: frequently
fruct. [fructus]: fruit
frust. [frustillatim]: bit by bit; in small bits
ft. [fiat or fiant]: let it be made; let them be made
ft. cataplasm. [fiat cataplasma]: let a poultice be made
ft. cerat. [fiat ceratum]: let a cerate be made
ft. chart. [fiant chartae]: let papers (or powders) be made
ft. collyr. [fiat collyrium]: let an eyewash be made
ft. confec. [fiat confectio]: let a confection be made
ft. elect. [fiat electuarium]: let an electuary be made
ft. emp. [fiat emplastrum]: let a plaster be made
ft. emuls. [fiat emulsum]: let an emulsion be made
ft. garg. [fiat gargarisma]: let a gargle be made
ft. haust. [fiat haustus]: let a draft be made
ft. infus. [fiat infusum]: let an infusion be made
ft. inject. [fiat injectio]: let an injection be made
ft. linim. [fiat linimentum]: let a liniment be made

ft. mas. [fiat massa]: let a lump or a mass be made
ft. mist. [fiat mistura]: let a mixture be made
ft. pil. [fiant pilulae]: let pills be made
ft. pulv. [fiat pulvis]: let a powder be made
ft. pulv. subtil. [fiat pulvis subtilis]: let a fine powder be made
ft. solut. [fiat solutio]: let a solution be made
ft. suppos. [fiant suppositoria]: let suppositories be made
ft. troch. [fiant trochisci]: let lozenges be made
ft. ung. [fiat unguentum]: let an ointment be made
ft. venaes. [fiat venaesectio]: let a vein be bled

G

g. [gutta]: a drop
g.g.g. [gummi gutti gambiae]: a gamboge
garg. [gargarisma]: a gargle
gel. quav. [gelatina quavis]: in any kind of jelly
gg. [guttae]: drops
glyc. or **glycer.** or **glyct.** [glyceritum]: glycerite
gossyp. [gossypium]: cotton
gr. [granum]: grain
grad. [gradatim]: gradually or by degrees
grat. [gratus]: pleasant; agreeable
grm. [gramma]: a gram
grn. [granum]: grain
gt. [gutta]: a drop
gtt. [guttae]: drops
gutt. [gutturi]: to or for the throat
gutt. appl. [gutturi applicandus]: to be applied to the throat
gutt. quibus. [guttis quibusdam]: with a few drops
guttat. [guttatim]: by drops; drop by drop

H

H. [hora]: hour
h.a. [hoc anno]: in this year
h.c. [honoris causa]: for the sake of honor
h.d. or **H.D.** [hora decubitus]: at bedtime
H.I. [hic iacet or hic jacet]: here lies

H.I.S. [hic iacet sepultus]: here lies buried
h.l. [hoc loco]: in this place
h.m. [hoc mense]: in this month
H.M.P. [hoc monumentum posuit]: he or she erected this monument
h.q. [hoc quaere]: look for this
H.S. [hic sepultus]: here [lies] buried
h.s. [hoc sensu]: in this sense
h.s. or **H.S.** [hora somni]: at bedtime
h.s.e. or **H.S.E.** [hic sepultus est]: here lies buried
h.t. [hoc tempore]: at this time
h.t. [hoc titulo]: under this title
hab. corp. [habeas corpus]: (leg.) a writ of habeas corpus
habt. [habeat]: let him or her have
hac noct. [hac nocte]: tonight; this night
haust. [haustus]: a draught; a drink
hebdom. [hebdomada]: a week; a seven-day period
her. [heres]: heir
Hg. or **hg.** [hydrargyrum]: mercury; quicksilver
hir. or **hirud.** [hirudo]: a leech
hoc vesp. [hoc vespere]: this evening
hor. [hora]: hour
hor. decub. [hora decubitus]: at bedtime
hor. interim. [horis intermediis]: at intermediate hours
hor. quad. or **hor. quadrant.** [horae quadrante]: a quarter of an hour
hor. un. spat. [horae unius spatio]: after one hour
hydr. [hydrargyrum]: mercury; quicksilver

I

i.a. [in absentia]: in absence
i.c. [inter cibos]: between meals
i.e. [id est]: that is
i.q. [idem quod]: the same as
ib. or **ibid.** [ibidem]: in the same place (e.g., in a book)
id. [idem]: the same; the same as above
ient. or **ientac.** [ientaculum or jentaculum]: breakfast
ign. [ignotus]: unknown
illic. [illico]: immediately
illinend. [illinendus]: to be smeared
impr. [imprimis]: first of all; first in order

in aur. dext. [in aurem dextram]: into the right ear
in aur. sinist. [in aurem sinistram]: into the left ear
in d. [in dies]: daily
in lim. [in limine]: in the beginning
in litt. [in litteris]: in correspondence
in ocul. dext. [in oculum dextrum]: into the right eye
in ocul. sinist. [in oculum sinistrum]: into the left eye
in pr. [in principio]: in the beginning
in pulm. [in pulmento]: in gruel
in sing. aur. [in singulas aures]: into each ear
in trans. [in transitu]: in transit; on the way
in ut. [in utero]: in the womb
in vit. [in vitro]: in a glass; in a test tube or petri dish
inc. [incide]: cut
inc. or **incis.** [incisus]: cut into pieces
ind. [indies]: daily
indet. [indeterminans]: unidentified
inf. [infra]: below
inf. [infunde]: pour in
inf. [infusio or infusum]: an infusion
infra dig. [infra dignitatem]: beneath one's dignity
infric. [infricetur]: let it be rubbed in
infus. [infusio or infusum]: an infusion
inhal. [inhaletur]: let it be inhaled
init. [initio]: in or at the beginning (referring to a passage in a book)
inj. enem. [injiciatur enema]: let an enema be injected
inj. hyp. [injectio hypodermica]: hypodermic injection
inj. or **inject.** [injectio]: an injection
inspir. [inspiretur]: let it be breathed (into)
instill. [instillentur]: let them be dropped in or into
instill. [instilletur]: let it be dropped in or into
insuff. [insufflatio]: an insufflation
int. [internus]: inward; internal
inter noct. [inter noctem]: during the night
inv. [invenit]: he or she designed it
involv. [involve]: roll; coat
iod. [iodinium or iodum]: iodine
iter. [iteretur]: let it be repeated
iux. [iuxta]: near; next to

J

jent. or **jentac.** [jentaculum or ientaculum]: breakfast
jug. [jugulo]: to or for the throat
jul. [julepum or julepus or julapium]: a julep
jusc. [jusculum]: juice; broth; soup
jux. [juxta]: near; next to

K

K. [kalium]: potassium
k. [kilometrum]: kilometer
kg. or **kilo.** [kilogramma]: kilogram
kilogra. [kilogramma]: kilogram
kl. [kilolitrum]: kiloliter

L

l. or **lib.** [libra; pl. libri]: a book
l. [litrum]: a liter
L.B. [lectori benevolo]: to the gentle reader
l.c. [loco citato]: in the place cited
L.S. [lectori salutem]: greetings to the reader
L.S. [locus sigilli]: the place of the seal
l.s.c. [loco supra citato]: in the place cited before
lac vac. [lac vaccinum]: cow's milk
lac v.d. [lac vaccinum defloratum]: skimmed cow's milk
laev. [laevus]: the left
lat. [latitudine]: in width
lat. [latus]: side; flank; broad; wide
lat. dol. [lateri dolenti]: to the painful side
latitud. [latitudine]: in width
lavat. [lavatio]: bathing; washing; also, a washing apparatus
lb. [libra or libra pondo]: a pound by weight
Li. [lithium]: lithium
lin. [linimentum]: a liniment
linct. [linctus]: a soothing cough syrup
liq. [liquor]: liquor; fluid; solution
lit. [litrum]: a liter

loc. cit. [loco citato]: in the place cited
loc. laud. [loco laudato]: in the place cited with approval
long. [longitudine]: in length
loq. [loquitur]: he or she speaks
lot. [lotio]: a lotion
lumb. [lumborum]: the loins

M

m. [mane]: morning; in the morning
m. [masculinus or masculinum]: masculine; manly
m. [masculus]: male; a man
m. [metrum]: a meter
m. [minimum]: a minim; a very small amount
m. et n. [mane et nocte]: morning and night
m. et v. [mane et vespere]: morning and evening
m. ft. m. [misce fiat mistura]: mix to make a mixture
m. ft. p. [misce fiat pulvis]: mix to make a powder
m. ft. pil. [misce fiant pilulae]: mix to make or form pills
m. or **M.** [meridies]: noon
m. or **M.** [misce]: mix
M.D. [Medicinae Doctor]: Doctor of Medicine
m.d. [more dicto]: as directed
m.d.s. [misce, detur, signetur]: mix, give, sign
m.m. [mutatis mutandis]: with the necessary changes being made
m.p. [male positus]: badly placed
m.p. [mane primo]: early in the morning
m.p. [massa pilularum]: a pill mass
m. pr. or **m. prim.** [mane primo]: early in the morning
m.s. [more solito]: in the usual manner
m.s. or **ms.** [manu scriptum]: written by hand (i.e., a manuscript)
m.s.a. [misce secundum artem]: mix according to practice
m. seq. [mane sequenti]: on the following morning
M.V. [Medicus Veterinarius]: a veterinarian
mac. [macera]: macerate
mag. [magnus]: large; great
mal. pos. [male positus]: badly placed
mas. or **mass.** [massa]: a mass
masc. [masculinus or masculinum]: masculine; manly

matut. [matutinus]: of the morning
mic. pan. [mica panis]: bread crumb
min. [minimum]: a minim; a very small amount
minut. [minutum or minutus]: a minute or small amount
mist. [mistura]: a mixture
mitt. [mittatur]: let it be sent; let it be drawn
mitt. [mitte]: send
mitt. sang. [mittatur sanguis]: let blood be drawn
mitt. tal. or **mit. tal.** [mitte tales]: send such
mittr. [mittatur]: let it be sent; let it be drawn
mod. praesc. [modo praescripto]: as prescribed or directed
more dict. [more dicto]: as directed
more sol. [more solito]: in the usual manner
MS [manuscriptus]: manuscript
MSS [manuscripta]: manuscripts

N

n. [natus]: born
n. [neutrum]: neuter
n. [nocte]: at night; in the night
N.B. or **n.b.** [nota bene]: note well
n. et m. [nocte et mane]: night and morning
n.l. [non licet]: it is not permitted
n.m. [nocte maneque]: night and morning
n.p. or **N.P.** [nomen proprium]: proper name
n.p.o. [nil per os]: nothing by mouth
n.t.s.n. or **ne tr. s. num.** [ne tradas sine nummo]: do not deliver unless paid
Na. [natrium]: sodium
ne rep. [ne repetatur]: do not repeat
nebul. [nebula]: a spray
nig. [niger]: black
No. or **no.** [numero]: in number
nom. [nomen; pl. nomina]: name
non obs. [non obstante]: notwithstanding
non rep. [non repetatur]: let it not be repeated (i.e., do not refill)
non seq. [non sequitur]: it does not follow
nuch. cap. [nucha capitis]: the nape of the neck

O

O or **O.** [octarius]: a pint
o. alt. h. [omni alterna hora]: every other hour
o.b. [omni bihora or omni bihorio]: every two hours
o.c. [opere citato]: in the work cited
o.d. [oculus dexter]: the right eye
o.d. [omne die]: all day; every day
o.h. [omni hora]: every hour
o.m. [omni mane]: every morning
o.n. [omni nocte]: every night
o.o. [oleum olivae]: olive oil
o.q.h. [omni quadranta hora]: every quarter hour
o.s. [oculus sinister]: the left eye
o.s.h. [omni singula hora]: every single hour
o. sext. h. [omni sexta hora]: every six hours
o. sing. h. [omni singula hora]: every single hour
o.u. [oculi uterque]: for both eyes
ob. [obiit]: he or she died
ob. [obiter]: incidentally
ob.s.p. [obiit sine prole]: he or she died without issue
oblat. [oblatum]: a cachet (e.g., a medicine capsule)
oct. [octarius]: a pint
ocul. [oculo]: to or for the eye
ol. [oleum]: oil
ol. ol. [oleum olivae]: olive oil
omn. [omnis]: all; every
omn. alt. hor. [omnibus alternis horis]: every other hour; at alternate hours
omn. bid. [omni biduo]: every two days
omn. bih. [omni bihora or omni bihorio]: every two hours
omn. die [omne die]: all day; every day
omn. hor. [omni hora]: every hour
omn. man. [omni mane]: every morning
omn. noc. [omni nocte]: every night
omn. quad. hor. [omni quadranta hora]: every quarter hour
op. [ope]: by means of
op. [opus]: a work
op. cit. [opere citato]: in the work cited
ope pen. [ope penicilli]: by means of a camel-hair brush

opt. [optimus]: the best
ov. [ovum]: an egg
ovi alb. [ovi albumen]: the egg white
ovi vit. [ovi vitellus]: the egg yolk
ovil. jus. [ovillum jusculum]: mutton broth
ox. or **oxy.** or **oxym.** [oxymel]: a mixture of honey, vinegar, and water
Oxon. [Oxoniensis]: of Oxford
oz. [uncia]: an ounce

P

. . . [placebo]: I will please (i.e., a prescription given to please a patient)
p. [pagina]: the page of a book or letter
p. [partim]: in part
P. [pondere]: by weight
P. or **pt.** [perstetur]: let it be continued
p.a. [parti affectae]: to the affected part
p.a. [partibus affectis]: to the affected parts
p.a. [per annum]: by the year
p.a.a. [parti affectae applicandus]: to be applied to the affected part
p.ae. [partes aequales]: in equal parts
p.c. [post cibos]: after meals
p.c. [post cibum]: after food
p. dol. [parti dolenti]: to the painful part
p.g. [persona grata]: an acceptable or welcome person
p.j. or **p. jent.** or **p. jentac.** [post jentaculum]: after breakfast
p.m. or **P.M.** [post meridiem]: after noon
p.m. or **P.M.** [post mortem]: after death
p.n.g. [persona non grata]: an unacceptable or unwelcome person
p.o. [per os]: by mouth; orally
p.p. [per procurationem]: by proxy; by the action of
p.p.a. or **P.P.A.** [phiala prius agitata]: after first shaking the bottle
p.r.a. [pro ratione aetatis]: according to age of the patient
p.r.n. or **P.R.N.** [pro re nata]: whenever necessary; as needed
P.P.S. or **PPS** [post postscriptum]: an additional postscript
P.S. or **PS** [post scriptum or postscriptum]: written after; a postscript
p.s.d.l. [post singulas dejectiones liquidas]: after each loose bowel movement
p.s.s.l. [post singulas sedes liquidas]: after each loose stool
p.t. [pro tempore]: for a time; temporarily

part. aff. [partem affectam]: affected part
part. dolent. [partem dolentem]: painful part
part. vic. [partibus vicibus or partitis vicibus]: in divided doses
parv. [parvus]: small
pas. or **pastil.** [pastillum or pastillus]: a small lozenge; a breath lozenge
pass. [passim]: throughout; here and there
paul. [paullum]: a little
paux. [pauxillum]: a very little
Pb. or **pb.** [plumbum]: lead
pct. [per centum]: by the hundred
pect. [pectori]: to the chest or breast
pect. [pectus]: the chest; breast
pedet. [pedetentim]: step by step; by degrees
pen. cam. [penicillum camelinum]: a camel's hair brush
pend. [pendens]: weighing; hanging
penicul. cam. [penicillum camelinum]: a camel's hair brush
per cent. or **p.c.** [per centum]: by the hundred
per pro. [per procurationem]: by proxy; by the action of
per salt. [per saltum]: by leaps; all at once
pess. [pessus]: a pessary; a vaginal suppository
Ph.D. [Philosophiae Doctor]: Doctor of Philosophy
Phar. D. or **Pharm. D.** [Pharmaciae Doctor]: Doctor of Pharmacy
pigm. [pigmentum]: pigment; paint
pil. [pilula]: a pill
pinx. [pinxit]: he or she painted this
pl. [pluralis]: plural
poc. [poculum]: a cup
pocill. [pocillum]: a small cup
pocul. [poculum]: a cup
poll. [pollex]: the thumb or big toe; an inch in length
poll. sex [pollices sex]: six inches (i.e., half a foot)
pone aur. [pone aurem]: put behind the ear
pot. [potio or potus]: a potion; a drink; a draught
pp. [paginae]: the pages of a book or letter
PPS [post postscriptum]: an additional postscript
ppt. [praecipitatus]: precipitated
praep. [praeparatus]: prepared
prand. [prandium]: lunch or dinner
prim. luc. [prima luce]: at first light; early in the morning
prim. m. [primo mane]: early in the morning

pro capill. [pro capillis]: for the hair
pro jug. [pro jugulo]: for the throat
pro ocul. [pro oculis]: for the eyes
pro ocul. dext. [pro oculo dextro]: for the right eye
pro ocul. laev. [pro oculo laevo]: for the left eye
pro pot. s. [pro potu sumendus]: to be taken as a drink
pro rat. aet. [pro ratione aetatis]: according to age of the patient
pro rect. [pro recto]: rectal
pro sing. ocul. [pro singulis oculis]: for each eye
pro tem. [pro tempore]: for a time; temporarily
pro ureth. [pro urethra]: urethral
pro vagin. [pro vagina]: vaginal
prox. [proximo]: the next; of or in the following month
prox. m. [proximo mense]: the next month
PS [post scriptum or postscriptum]: a postscript
pt. [perstetur]: let it be continued
pt. aeq. [partes aequales]: in equal parts
ptc. [participium]: a participle
pulv. [pulveres]: powders
pulv. [pulvis]: a powder
pulv. consper. [pulvis conspersus]: a dusting powder
pxt. [pinxit]: he or she painted this
pyx. [pyxis]: a pill box

Q

q. alt. h. [quaque alterna hora]: every other hour
q.d. [quasi dicat]: as much as to say
q.d. [quasi dictum]: as if said
q.d. [quater die]: four times a day
q.e. [quod est]: which is
Q.E.D. or **q.e.d.** [quod erat demonstrandum]: which was to be demonstrated or proven
Q.E.F. or **q.e.f.** [quod erat faciendum]: which was to be done
q.h. [quaque hora]: every hour
q.i.d. [quater in die]: four times a day
q.l. [quantum libet]: as much as you please
q. lib. [quantum libet]: as much as you please
q.m. or **Q.M.** [quaque mane]: every morning
q.n. [quaque nocte]: every night

q.o.s. [quoties opus sit]: as often as required
q.p. [quantum placet]: as much as you please
q. pl. [quantum placet]: as much as you please
q.s. [quantum sufficit or quantum sufficiat]: as much as suffices
q.s. or **Q.S.** [quantum satis]: as much as satisfies
q.s.h. [quaque singula hora]: every single hour
q. sext. h. [quaque sexta hora]: every six hours
q. sing. h. [quaque singula hora]: every single hour
q.v. [quantum vis or quantumvis]: as much as you will
q.v. [quod vide]: (sing.) which see
q. vol. or **q.v.** [quantum volueris]: as much as you wish
qq. hor. [quaque hora]: every hour
qq. or **Qq.** [quaque]: each; every
qq. or **Qq.** [quoque]: also; too
qq.v. [quae vide]: (pl.) which see
qt. [quantitas]: quantity
qt. dupx. [quantitas duplex]: twice the amount
qt. dx. [quantitas duplex]: twice the amount
qu. [quaere]: a question or query
quant. suff. [quantum sufficit or quantum sufficiat]: as much as suffices
quart. hor. [quartis horis]: every four hours
quin. vel sex. in d. [quinquies vel sexies in die]: five or six times a day
quot. [quotidie]: daily
quot. op. sit [quoties opus sit]: as often as required
quotid. [quotidie]: daily

R

R. [regina]: queen
R. [rex]: king
R.I.P. [requiescat in pace]: may he or she rest in peace
R.I.P. [requiescit in pace]: he or she rests in peace
r. in p. [redigatur in pulverem]: let it be reduced to a powder
rec. [recens]: recent; fresh
red. in pulv. [redigatur in pulverem]: let it be reduced to a powder
red. in pulv. [reductus in pulverem]: reduce to a powder
reg. hepat. [regio hepatis]: the region of the liver
reg. umbil. [regio umbilici]: the umbilical region
reli. or **reliq.** [reliquum or reliquus]: the rest; the remaining; the remainder

rep. [repetatur]: let it be repeated
repet. or **rept.** [repetatur]: let it be repeated
℞ [recipe]: take

S

s̄ s̄ [semis]: half or one half
S. [sepultus]: buried
S. [signa]: write or mark thus on the prescription label
s. [signetur]: let it be written; label it thus
s. [spiritus]: spirit; an alcoholic drink; a spirit of any kind
S. or **s.** [sulfur or sulphur]: sulfur
s.a. or **S.A.** [secundum artem]: according to pharmaceutical practice
s.a. [sine anno]: without date
s.d. [semel die]: once a day
s.d. [sine die]: indefinitely
s.i.d. or **S.I.D.** [semel in die]: once a day
s.l. [sine loco]: without place
s.l.a. [sine loco et anno]: without place and year
s.l.a.n. [sine loco, anno, vel nomine]: without place, year, or name
s.n. or **S.N.** [secundum naturam]: according to nature; naturally
s.n. [sine nomine]: anonymous
s.n.p. [signetur nomine proprio]: label with proper name
s.n.v. [si non valeat]: if it does not respond
s.o.s. or **si op. sit** [si opus sit]: if necessary; if occasion requires
s.p. [sine prole]: without issue
S.P.Q.R. [Senatus Populusque Romanus]: The Senate and the People of Rome (motto of Rome)
s.p.s. [sine prole supersite]: without surviving issue
s.s. [sine sale]: without salt
s.s.s. or **S.S.S.** [stratum super stratum]: layer upon layer
s.v. [spiritus vini]: wine spirit; an alcoholic spirit
s.v. [sub verbo]: under the word or heading
s.v. [sub voce]: under the word or heading
s.v.g. [spiritus vini Gallici]: brandy
s.v.p. [si vires permittant]: if strength permits
s.v.r. [spiritus vini rectificatus]: rectified wine spirit; alcohol
s.v.t. [spiritus vini tenuis]: proof spirit
sacch. [saccharatus]: sugarcoated
sacch. [saccharum]: sugar; cane sugar

Sal. or **S.** [Salutem dicit!]: Greetings!
sc. [scilicet]: namely; to wit; that is to say
sc. [sculpsit]: he or she carved or engraved it
scat. [scatula]: a box
scil. [scilicet]: namely; to wit; that is to say
scr. [scrupulus or scrupulum]: a scruple
scrob. cord. [scrobiculo cordis]: to the pit of the stomach
sculpt. [sculpsit]: he or she carved or engraved it
sec. [secundum]: according to
sec. art. [secundum artem]: according to pharmaceutical practice
sec. hor. [secundis horis]: every two hours
sec. leg. [secundum legem]: according to law
sec. nat. [secundum naturam]: naturally
sec. reg. [secundum regulam]: according to rule
sem. die [semel die]: once a day
sem. in die [semel in die]: once a day
semidr. [semidrachma]: half a drachm (dram)
semih. [semihora]: half an hour
seq. [sequens]: (sing.) the following
seq. [sequitur]: it follows
seqq. [sequentia]: (pl.) the following
sesquih or **sesqh.** [sesquihora]: an hour and a half
sesunc. [sesuncia]: an ounce and a half
sex. d. [sexies die]: six times a day
sex. in d. [sexies in die]: six times a day
sext. hor. [sextis horis]: every six hours
sg. or **sing.** [singularis]: singular
si dol. urg. [si dolor urgeat]: if the pain is severe
si non val. [si non valeat]: if it does not respond
si vir. perm. [si vires permittant]: if strength permits
Sig. [signa]: write or mark thus on the prescription label
sig. [signetur]: let it be written; label it thus
sig. nom. prop. [signetur nomine proprio]: label with proper name
sigill. [sigillum]: seal; signet
sinap. [sinapis]: mustard
sing. [singulorum]: of each
sing. auror. [singulis auroris]: every morning
sing. hor. [singulis horis]: every hour
sinist. [sinister]: left
Sn. or **sn.** [stannum]: tin

sol. [solutio or solutum]: a solution
solv. [solve]: dissolve
solv. c̄ cal. [solve cum calore]: dissolve by warming
sp. nov. [species novum]: a new species
spirit. vin. [spiritus vini]: wine spirit; an alcoholic spirit
spr. [spiritus]: spirit; an alcoholic drink; a spirit of any kind
st. [stet]: let it stand
stat. [statim]: immediately
stern. [sterno]: to the chest
sub. [subaudi]: to read between the lines
sug. [sugatur]: let it be sucked
sum. [sumantur]: let them be taken
sum. [sumat]: let him or her take
sum. [sume or sumatur]: take or let it be taken
sum. tal. [sumat talem]: take one such
sup. [supra]: above
sup. cit. [supra citato]: cited above
sup. gossyp. [super gossypium]: upon cotton wool
sup. lin. [super linteum]: upon linen
supp. or **suppos.** [suppositorium]: a suppository
syr. [syrupus]: a syrup
syr. fus. [syrupus fuscus]: molasses

T

t. [tempore]: in the time of
t. [tinctura]: tincture; a dye
t.i.d. or **T.I.D.** [ter in die]: three times a day
t. in hebdom. [ter in hebdomada]: three times a week
t.q.d. [ter quaterve die]: three or four times a day
tab. [tabella]: a tablet
tal. [talis]: such
tal. dos. [tales doses]: such doses
tars. ocul. [tarsis oculorum]: to the eyelids
temp. [tempore]: in the time of
ter in hebdom. [ter in hebdomada]: three times a week
ter in hor. [ter in hora]: three times an hour
ter quot. [ter quotidie]: three times daily
ter. [tere]: rub; triturate
ter. bene sim. [tere bene simul]: rub together well

tert. hor. [tertiis horis]: every three hours
thorac. [thoraci]: to the chest
tinct. [tinctura]: tincture; a dye
tot. quot. [toties quoties]: as often as; repeatedly; on each occasion
TR [tinctura]: a tincture; a dye
trid. [triduum]: a period of three days
troch. [trochiscus]: a lozenge
tunic. [tunicetur]: let it be coated
tunic. c̄ gelat. [tunicentur cum gelatino]: let them be gelatin-coated
tunic. pil. [tunicentur pilulae]: let the pills be coated
tunicat. [tunicatus]: coated
tus. [tussis]: a cough
tuss. ingrav. [tussi ingravescente]: with the cough growing worse
tuss. mol. [tussi molesta]: with the cough being troublesome
tuss. mol. [tussis molestante]: the cough being troublesome
tuss. urg. [tussi urgente]: with the cough being severe

U

u.i. [ubi infra]: in the place mentioned below
u.s. [ubi supra]: in the place mentioned above
u.t.i.d. [unam ter in die]: one three times a day
ult. [ultimo]: the last or previous month
ult. [ultimus]: the last
ult. m. [ultimo mense]: the last or previous month
ult. praesc. or **ult. praes.** [ultimo praescriptus]: last prescribed; the last ordered
unc. [uncia]: an ounce
ung. or **ungt.** [unguentum]: an ointment
usq. [usque]: as far as
ut dict. [ut dictum]: as directed
ut inf. [ut infra]: as stated or shown below
ut sup. [ut supra]: as stated or shown above
ux. [uxor]: wife

V

v. [vide]: see
v. or **vo.** [verso]: reverse side
v. or **vol.** [volumen]: volume

v. or **vs.** [versus]: against
v.a. [vixit . . . annos]: he or she lived . . . years
v.g. [verbi gratia]: for example
v.i. [vide infra]: see below
v.o.s. [vitello ovi solutus]: dissolve in egg yolk
v.s. [vide supra]: see above
v.v. [vice versa]: conversely
vehic. [vehiculum]: a vehicle; a means of conveyance
venaes. [venaesectio]: bleeding; venesection (i.e., bloodletting)
verb. sap. [verbum sapienti]: a word to the wise
verb. sat or **verb. sat sap.** [verbum sat sapienti (est)]: a word to the wise is sufficient
vesp. [vesper]: evening
vesp. [vesperi]: in or of the evening
vet. [veteres]: the ancients; forefathers
vic. [vices]: time; times; turn
vin. [vinum]: wine
vir. or **virid.** [viridis]: green
viz. [videlicet]: namely; to wit
volvend. [volvendus]: to be rolled
vom. fin. [vomitu finito]: the vomiting having ceased
vom. urg. [vomitione urgente]: the vomiting becoming serious
vomit. [vomitio]: the act of vomiting
vs. [venaesectio]: bleeding; venesection (i.e., bloodletting)

X

xer. [xericus]: sherry

Z

Zn. [zincum]: zinc
zz. [zingiber]: ginger

Miscellanea (Miscellaneous)

Some Common Prepositions and Particles

a or **ab**: from; by
ad: to; at; up to
ambo: both
ante: before
anti: against; opposed to
apo: from; away from
apud: at; near; by; next to
bis: twice
circa: about; near; around
circum: around; about
cis or **citra**: this side of; within
contra: against
coram: before; in the presence of
cui: to whom
cum: with
de: of; concerning; from
donec: until
dum: while
durante: during
e or **ex**: from; out of
ergo: therefore
et: and; also
extra: without; outside of; in addition to
hic, **hac**, **hoc**: this
ibi: there
in: in; into
infra: below; beneath
inter: between; among
intra: inside; within
juxta (iuxta): near; next to; according to
nisi: unless
non: no; not
ob: for; on account of
omne (**omnis**): all
ope: by means of
per: by; through
pone: behind
post: after
prae (**pre**): before
praeter: in front of; beyond
pro: for; before; on behalf of
prope: near
propter: because of; on account of
qua: as
quasi: as if
re: regarding; concerning
retro: behind; backward
secundum: according to
semis: half; one-half
semper: always
si: if; supposing that
sic: thus; so
sine: without
sub: under
super: over; above
supra: over; above
totus: all; the whole
trans: across; through
ubi: where
ultra: beyond

DOI: 10.4324/9781003255352-4

ne: lest; not
nec: neither; not
nihil or **nil**: nothing
usque ad: up to; as far as
ut: as; so that
vel: or

Some Common Prefixes

a- or **an-** without
ab- away from
ad- toward; near
ante- before
anti- against
auto- self
bi- two, twice
bis- two; twice
bin- two
circum- around
contra- against
di- twice; two
dia- through
dis- twice; two
duo- two
epi- on; upon
eu- good
ex- out of
extra- outside of
hemi- one-half
hepta- seven; seventh
hetero- other
hexa- six; sixth
homo- same
hyper- above; beyond
hypo- below; under
inter- between; among
intra- within
macro- large
medi- middle
mega- large
meta- beyond; altered
micro- small
mon- one
mono- one
multi- many
neo- new
non- not
ortho- correct; straight
para- beyond
penta- five; fifth
per- through; beyond
peri- around
poly- many
post- after
prae- (**pre-**) before
proto- before; first; lower
pseudo- false
pyro- changed by heat
quadra- four; fourth
quadri- four; fourth
retro- backward; behind
semi- half
sesqui- one and one half
sub- below; under
super- above
supra- above
sym-/syn- with; together
ter- three
tetra- four
toxi- poisonous
tri- (**tris-**) three; three times
ultra- beyond
un- one
uni- single
xanth- yellow

Some Useful Medical Directives

addendus: to be added
adhibendus: to be applied
ammoniatus: ammoniated
applicandus: to be applied
bibendus: to be drunk
bulliens: boiling
calcinatus: burnt
calefaciens: warming
capiendus: to be taken
carbolisatus: carbolized
compositus: compound
compressus: compressed
conspersus: sprinkled
contusus: bruised
dandus: to be given
deglutiendus: to be swallowed
delendus: to be left out
demulcens: demulcent
destillatus: distilled
dilutus: diluted
dividendus: to be divided
exoneratus: relieved
expressus: pressed or squeezed out
exsiccatus: thoroughly dried
extendendus: to be spread
fervidus: to be boiling hot
foratus: pierced
formandus: to be formed
fumans: fuming
infricandus: to be rubbed in
instillandus: to be dropped in
liquefactus: liquefied
miscendus: to be mixed
mittendus: to be sent
omittendus: to be omitted
promovendus: induced
pulveratus: powdered
purificatus: purified; refined
recipe: take
rectificatus: rectified
repetendus: to be repeated
roborans: strengthening
saturatus: saturated
servandus: to be preserved
statim: immediately
sumendus: to be taken
tritus: rubbed
utendus: to be used

The Latin Calendar

The Calendar Year (Mensis)

Januarius: January
Februarius: February
Martius: March
Aprilis: April
Maius: May
Iunius: June
Quinctilis or **Iulius**: July (after Julius Caesar)
Sextilis or **Augustus**: August (after Caesar Augustus)

Januarii: in January
Februarii: in February
Martii: in March
Aprilis: in April
Maii: in May
Junii: in June
Julii: in July
Augusti: in August

September: September	**Septembris**: in September
October: October	**Octobris**: in October
November: November	**Novembris**: in November
December: December	**Decembris**: in December

The Calendar Month

Idus [the Ides]: the fifteenth day in March, May, July, and October; the thirteenth day in all other months

Kalendae or **Calendae** [the Kalends or Calends]: the first day of a Roman month

Nonae [the Nones]: the seventh day in March, May, July, and October; the fifth day in all other months

The Days of the Week (Septimana)

Dies Solis or **Dies Dominica**: Sunday	**Die Soli**: on Sunday
Dies Lunae: Monday	**Die Lunae**: on Monday
Dies Martis: Tuesday	**Die Martis**: on Tuesday
Dies Mercurii: Wednesday	**Die Mercurii**: on Wednesday
Dies Iovis/Jovis: Thursday	**Die Iovis/Jovis**: on Thursday
Dies Veneris: Friday	**Die Veneris**: on Friday
Dies Saturni: Saturday	**Die Saturni**: on Saturday
Dies Sabbati: the Sabbath day	**Die Sabbati**: on the Sabbath day

Roman Numerals

CARDINALS	ORDINALS
unus (I): one	**primus**: first
duo (II): two	**secundus**, **alter**: second
tres (III): three	**tertius**: third
quattuor/quatuor (IIII, IV): four	**quartus**: fourth
quinque (V): five	**quintus**: fifth
sex (VI): six	**sextus**: sixth
septem (VII): seven	**septimus**: seventh
octo (VIII): eight	**octavus**: eighth
novem (VIIII, IX): nine	**nonus**: ninth
decem (X): ten	**decimus**: tenth
undecim (XI): eleven	**undecimus**: eleventh

duodecim (XII): twelve	**duodecimus**: twelfth
tredecim (XIII): thirteen	**tertius decimus**: thirteenth
quattuordecim (XIIII, XIV): fourteen	**quartus decimus**: fourteenth
quindecim (XV): fifteen	**quintus decimus**: fifteenth
sedecim (or **sexdecim**) (XVI): sixteen	**sextus decimus**: sixteenth
septendecim (XVII): seventeen	**septimus decimus**: seventeenth
duodevinginti (or **octodecim**) (XVIII): eighteen	**duodevicesimus** (or **octavusdecimus**): eighteenth
undeviginti (or **novemdecim**) (XIIII, XIX): nineteen	**undevicesimus** (or **novemdecimus**): nineteenth
viginti (XX): twenty	**vicesimus**: twentieth
unus et viginti (XXI) (or **viginti unus**): twenty-one	**vicesimus primus** (or **unus et vicesimus**): twenty-first
duo et viginti (or **viginti duo**) (XXII): twenty-two	**vicesimus secundus** (or **duo et vicesimus** or **alter et vicemus**): twenty-second
duodetriginta (XXVIII): twenty-eight	**duodetricesimus**: twenty-eighth
undetriginta (XXIX): twenty-nine	**undetricesimus**: twenty-ninth
triginta (XXX): thirty	**tricesimu**s: thirtieth
duodequadraginta (XXXVIII): thirty-eight	**duodequadragesimus**: thirty-eighth
undequadraginta (XXXIX): thirty-nine	**undequadragesimus**: thirty-ninth
quadraginta (XL): forty	**quadragesimus**: fortieth
duodequinquaginta (XLVIII): forty-eight	**duodequinquagesimus**: forty-eighth
undequinquaginta (XLIX): forty-nine	**undequinquagesimus**: forty-ninth
quinquaginta (L): fifty	**quinquagesimus**: fiftieth
sexaginta (LX): sixty	**sexagesimus**: sixtieth
septuaginta (LXX): seventy	**septuagesimus**: seventieth
octoginta (LXXX): eighty	**octogesimus**: eightieth
nonaginta (XC): ninety	**nonagesimus**: ninetieth
centum (C): one hundred	**centesimus**: the hundredth
centum (et) unus (CCI): one hundred and one	**centesimus (et) primus**: hundred and first

ducenti (CC): two hundred
ducenti quinquagenta (CCL or E): two hundred and fifty
trecenti (CCC): three hundred
quadringenti (CD): four hundred
quingenti (D): five hundred
sescenti (DC): six hundred
septingenti (DCC): seven hundred
octingenti (DCCC): eight hundred
nongenti (DM): nine hundred
mille (M): one thousand
duo milia (MM): two thousand

ducentesimus: two hundredth
ducentesimus (et) quinquagesimus: two hundredth and fiftieth
trecentesimus: three hundredth
quadringentesimus: four hundredth
quingentesimus: five hundredth
sescentesimus: six hundredth
septingentesimus: seven hundredth
octingentesimus: eight hundredth
nongentesimus: nine hundredth
millesimus: one thousandth
bis millesimus: two thousandth

Some Apothecary Weights and Measures

centimetrum cubicum (**c.c.**): a cubic centimeter
congius (**C** or **cong.**): a gallon
drachma (ʒ or **dr.** or **dram.**): a dram
fluidrachma (**f**ʒ or **fldr.**): a fluiddram
gramma (**gm.**): a gram
granum (**gr.**): a grain
gutta (**g.** or **gt.**): a drop
guttae (**gtt.**): drops
kilogramma (**Kg.**): a kilogram
libra (**lb.**): a pound
litrum (**L.**): a liter
milligramma (**mg.**): a milligram
millilitrum (**mil.**): a milliliter
minimum (**♏.** or **min.**): a minim
octarius (**O** or **oct.**): a pint
scrupulus (℈ or **scr.**): a scruple
semis (s̅ s̅): half or one-half
uncia (℥ or **oz.** or **unc.**): an ounce

Some Elements on the Periodic Table

Aluminum or **Aluminium** (**Al**): Aluminum
Antimonium or **Stibium** (**Sb**): Antimony
Argentium (**Ag**): Silver
Arsenum or **Arsenicum** (**As**): Arsenic
Aurum (**Au**): Gold
Barium (**Ba**): Barium
Bismuthum (**Bi**): Bismuth
Cuprum (**Cu**): Copper
Ferrum (**Fe**): Iron
Hydrargyrum (**Hg**): Mercury
Hydrogenium (**H**): Hydrogen
Iodum (**I**): Iodine
Lithium (**Li**): Lithium
Magnesium (**Mg**): Magnesium
Manganum (**Mn**): Manganese
Oxygenium (**O**): Oxygen
Plumbum (**Pb**): Lead

Bromum (**Br**): Bromine
Cadmium (**Cd**): Cadmium
Calcium (**Ca**): Calcium
Carboneum (**C**): Carbon
Cerium (**Ce**): Cerium
Chlorum (**Cl**): Chlorine
Chromium (**Cr**): Chromium
Potassium or **Kalium** (**K**): Potassium
Sodium or **Natrium** (**Na**): Sodium
Strontium (**Sr**): Strontium
Sulfur or **Sulphur** (**S**): Sulfur
Zincum (**Zn**): Zinc

Varieties of Primary and Secondary Colors

albus: white
ater: black; dull black
atropurpureus: dark purple
aurantius/aurantiacus: orange
caeruleus: blue
caesicius: a bluish-grey
caesius: blue-grey
candidus: bright white
canus: a whitish-grey
cinereus: grey; ashen grey
coccineus: scarlet
croceus: saffron yellow
crocinus: golden yellow
flavus: yellow
fulvus: brown
fuscus: dusky brown
galbinus: greenish-yellow
glaucus: green-grey
luridus: pale yellow
luteus: yellow
niger: black
puniceus: pink
purpureus: purple
ruber: red
suffuscus: dark brown
viola/violaceus: violet
viridis: green
xanthus: yellow

Selected Medical and Botanical Place Names

Abyssinicus: Abyssinian
Africanus: African
Alpinus: Alpine

Americanus: American
Anglicus: English
Angolensis: Angolan
Antarcticus: of Antarctica
Arabicus: Arabic
Barbadensis: of Barbados
Brasiliensis: Brazilian
Britannicus: British
Bulgaricus: Bulgarian
Italicus: Italian
Jamaicensis: Jamaican
Japonicus: Japanese (see also, **Nipponensis**)
Judaicus (or **Iudaicus**): Jewish
Kentuckiensis: Kentuckian
Lapponicus: Laplandic
Londinensis: of London
Madagascariensis: of Madagascar
Malabaricus: of Malabar
Marilandicus: of Maryland
Mauretanicus: Mauretanian
Monspeliensis: from Montpelier

Burgundicus: Burgundian
Californicus: Californian

Cambricus: Welsh
Canadensis: Canadian

Cantabrigiensis: of Cambridge
Carolinensis: Carolinian
Chiliensis: Chilean
Chinensis: Chinese
Colchicus: Georgian
Coloniensis: of Cologne
Damascenus: of Damascus
Dublinensis: of Dublin
Edinensis/Edinburgensis: of Edinburgh
Europaeus: European
Florentinus: Florentine
Formosanus: Formosan (Taiwanese)
Gallicus: Gallic (French)
Germanicus: German
Helveticus: Swiss
Hibernicus: Irish

Indicus: Indian

Neomexicanus: New Mexican
Nipponensis: Japanese (see also, **Japonicus**)
Novaeanglicae: of New England
Novaehollandiae (New Holland): of Australia
Novaeseelandiae: of New Zealand
Noveboracensis: of New York
Norvegicus: Norwegian
Oxoniensis: of Oxford
Parisiensis: of Paris
Persica: Persian
Peruvianus: Peruvian
Philippinensis: of The Philippines
Ponticus: Pontus (now central Turkey)
Purshianus: Persian
Rossicus: Russian
Sinensis: Chinese

Syriacus: Syrian
Taurinensis: of Turin
Victoriae: Victorian
Virginiana or **Virginicus**: Virginian
Zeylanicus: of Ceylon

English-Latin Index

DOI: 10.4324/9781003255352-5

birthwort: **aristolochia**
bit by bit: **frustillatim**
bite: **morsus**
bitter: **acerbus** or **amarus**
bitter apple: **colocynthis**
bitter orange: **aurantium amarus**
bitterness: **amarities**
black: **ater** or **niger**
black and white: **atra et alba**
black currant: **ribes nigrum**
black pepper: **piper nigrum**
blackberry: **rubus villosus** (**rubus**) or **nigrobaccus**
blackened: **attinctus** or **denigratus**
bladder: **vesica**
bleeding: **venaesectio**
blemish: **macula**
blessed thistle: **cnicus benedictus**
blind: **caecus**
blind spot: **punctum caecum**
blister: **pustula**
blister burn: **bulla**
blistering: **vesicans** or **rubefaciens** or **epispasticus**
blood: **sanguis**
blood clot: **crassamentum**
blood plasma: **liquor sanguinis**
blood-stained: **cruentus**
bloodless: **exsanguis**
bloodletting: **venaesectio**
bloodroot: **sanguinaria**
bloodshot: **sanguine suffusus**
bloodsucker: **sanguisuga**
bloody urine: **mictus cruentus** or **sanguinis mictus**
blotting paper: **charta bibula**
blue: **caeruleus**
blueberry: **vaccinium**
bodily ills: **dolores corporis**
bodily strength: **vires corporis**
body: **corpus**
boil: **coque**
boiled: **coctus**
boiling: **bulliens** or **coctio**
boiling hot: **fervidus**
boiling water: **aqua bulliens**
bone: **os**
bone decay: **caries**
bone splinter: **spicula**
bones: **ossa**
bony: **osseus**
book: **codex**
born: **natus**
both: **ambo**
bottle: **phiala**
bottle (corked): **phiala suberata**
bottle (sealed): **phiala obturata**
bottom: **basis** or **fundus**
bougie: **bougium** or **bacillum**
bound together: **consolidus**
bowels: **alvus**
box: **scatula**
box of pills: **scatula pilularum**
boxwood: **buxus**
boy: **puer**
brandy: **spiritus vini Gallici** or **vini Gallici spiritus**
brass: **aes**
bread: **panis**
bread crumb: **mica panis** or **panis mica**
breakfast: **ientaculum/ jentaculum**
breaking wind: **crepitus**
breast: **pectus** or **mamma** or **mamilla**

breastbone: **os pectoris** or **sternum**
brimstone: **sulfur** or **sulphur**
bristle: **seta**
broad: **latus**
broken: **fractus**
broken in pieces: **comminutus**
bronze: **aes**
bronze-covered: **aeratus**
broom: **scoparius**
broth: **brodium**
brother: **frater**
brown sugar (brown): **saccharum fuscum**:
bruised: **contusus**
brush: **penicillum** or **peniculus**
buckthorn: **rhamnus cathartica** (**rhamnus**) or **frangula**
bud: **gemma** or **germen**
buffered: **buffera**
bull: **taurus**
burdock: **arctium lappa** (**lappa**)
buried: **sepultus**
burnt: **ustus** or **adustus**
burst open: **ruptus**
but: **sed**
butter: **butyrum**
buttermilk: **lac vaccinum butyricum**
butternut: **julans**
buttocks: **nates**
buttocks muscle: **gluteus maximus**
buzzing in the ears: **bombus**
by accident: **per infortunium**
by birth: **natu**
by biting: **mordicus**
by degrees: **sensim** or **tractim**
by force: **per vim**
by itself: **per se**
by night: **noctu** or **nocturnus**
by rubbing: **tritu**
by sipping: **sorbilo**
by the day: **per diem**
by the roots: **raditicus**
by turns: **invicem**
by weight: **pondere**

C

cabbage: **brassica**
cacao tree: **theobroma**
cachet: **oblatum**
caffeine: **caffeina**
Calabar bean: **physostigma**
calf: **vitulus**
camel's hair brush: **penicillum camelinum**
Canadian hemp: **apocynum**
Canadian snake root: **asarum canadense**
cancer: **cancer**
cancerous: **phagedaenicus**
canker sore: **cancrum oris**
canine teeth: **dentes cuspidati**
capsule: **capsula**
caraway: **carum**
carbon dioxide: **acidum aereum**
carbonated water: **aqua aerata**
carbuncle: **caruncula**
cardamom: **elettaria**
care: **cura**
cartilage: **cartilago**
cash on delivery (c.o.d.): **ne tradas sine nummo**
castor plant: **ricinus**
cat: **felis**
cataract: **glaucoma** or **caligo lentis**
catnip: **nepeta cataria** (**cataria**)

D

decaying: **tabidus**
deceased: **demortuus**
decoction: **decoctio** or **decoctum**
deep breath: **suspirium**
deep sleep: **sopor**
deep-seated: **profundus**
deep-vein thrombosis: **phlegmasia cerulea dolens**
deformity: **deformitas**
dehydrated: **dehydratus**
delay: **dilatio** or **mora**
delirium tremens: **mania a potu**
dementia from drinking: **dementia a potu**
deodorized: **deodoratus**
departure from life: **excessus e vita**
depilatory: **depilatorium**
dermatological: **dermatologicus**
dessert: **epidipnis**
diagnostic: **diagnosticus**
diarrhea: **diarrhoea**
died: **obiit**
diet: **diaeta**
digestive: **digestivus** or **pepticus**
dill: **anethum**
diluted: **dilutus** or **dilutum** or **tenuis**
dimple: **gelasinus**
dinner: **prandium**
dirty: **luteus**
discretion: **prudentia**
disease: **morbus**
dislocated: **luxus**
dispense: **dispensa**
dispensed quickly: **cito dispensatur**
dissolve: **solve**
dissolved: **solutus**
distilled: **destillatus**
distilled spirit: **aqua vitae**
distilled water: **aqua destillata** or **aqua pura** or **hydrolatum**
ditch: **fossa**
diuretic: **diureticus**
divided: **partitus**
dizziness: **vertigo**
do not admit: **ne admittas**
do not repeat: **ne repetatur**
do not repeat (refill): **non repetatur**
Doctor of Medicine: **Medicinae Doctor**
Doctor of Pharmacy: **Pharmaciae Doctor**
Doctor of Philosophy: **Philosophiae Doctor**
Doctor of Veterinarian Science: **Medicus Veterinarius**
dog: **canis**
dog tooth: **dens canis**
dogbane: **apocynum**
dogwood: **cornus**
domestic: **domesticus**
dose: **dosis**
double boiler: **balneum Mariae**
doubtful: **dubius**
dove: **columba** or **columbus**
downy: **plumeus**
dozen: **duodecim**
draught: **haustus**
dream: **somnium**
dregs: **faex**
dried: **aridus** or **siccatus** or **exsiccatus**
drink (n.): **potio** or **potus**
drink (v.): **bibe**
drinkable: **sorbilis**
drop by drop: **guttatim**
drops: **guttae**

dropsy: **aqua intercus** or **hydrops**
drowsiness: **stupor**
drowsy: **somnolentus**
drug: **medicamen** or **medicamentum**
drugged: **medicatus**
druggist: **pharmacopola** or **medicamentarius**
drugstore: **apotheca**
drunk: **ebrius**
dry: **siccus**
DTs: **delirium tremens**
duct: **ductus** or **vas**
dung: **stercus**
during: **durante**
during dinner: **inter cenam**
dwarf: **pumilio** or **pumilus**
dwarf-sized: **pygmaeus**
dyed: **tinctoreus**
dying: **moribundus**
dysentery: **dysentericus**

E

each: **quaque**
ear: **auris**
ear doctor: **medicus auricularius**
ear drops: **auristillae** or **otoguttae**
ear drum: **tympanum**
ear suppository: **aurinarium**
ear wax: **cerumen**
earlobe: **auricula**
early morning: **luce prima**
ears: **aures**
earth: **terra**
eastern: **orientalis**
easy: **facilis**
easy to please: **placabilis**
eau de Cologne: **aqua Coloniensis** or **spiritus Coloniensis**
edible: **edulis** or **esculentus**
effective: **efficiens**
effervescent: **effervescens**
egg: **ovum**
egg white: **ovi albumen**
egg yolk: **ovi vitellus** (**vitellus**)
egg-shaped: **ovatus**
eggshell: **ovi putamen** or **testa ovi**
eight: **octo**
elastic: **elasticus**
elbow: **ulna** or **cubitum**
elder tree: **sambucus**
elm: **ulmus**
emergency: **subitum**
enamel: **dentium cortex**
enough: **satis**
epidemic: **epidemicus**
epilepsy: **morbus caducas** or **morbus comitialis** or **sacer morbis**
Epsom salt: **sal amarus** or **sal catharticus** or **magnesiae sulphas/magnesii sulphatis**
equal: **aequalis**
erysipelas: **sacer ignis** or **ignis sacer** or **ignis sancti Antonii**
ether: **aether**
ethereal: **aethereus**
evaporating dish: **patina**
evening: **vesper**
evergreen: **sempervirens**
every: **omnis**
every day (everyday): **cotidie** or **cotidianus** or **quotidianus**
every hour: **omni hora** or **quaque hora** or **singulis horis**
every morning: **omni mane** or **quaque mane** or **singulis auroris**

every night: **omni nocte** or **quaque nocte**
example: **exemplum**
excrement: **merda**
external: **externus**
extract: **extractum**
eye: **oculus**
eye doctor: **medicus ocularius**
eye drops: **oculoguttae**
eye ointment: **oculentum**
eye teeth: **dentes cuspidati**
eyebrow: **supercilium**
eyelash: **cilium**
eyelashes: **cilia**
eyelid: **cilium** or **palpebra**
eyelids: **tarsi oculorum**
eyes: **oculi**
eyewash: **collyrium**

F

face: **facies** or **vultus**
fainting spell: **syncope** or **defectio animi** or **defectum animae**
faith: **fides**
false cardamom: **alpinia nutans**
false or wild indigo: **baptisia**
fasting: **esuriens** or **impransus**
fat: **adeps**
fat (size): **obesus**
father: **pater**
fatty: **pinguis**
favor: **gratis**
fear of water: **hydrophobia**
fearful: **timidus**
feather: **penna** or **pluma**
feathered: **pennatus**
feeler: **tentaculum**
feet: **pedes**
female: **femina**
female pubic region: **mons veneris**
female reproductive system: **pudenda muliebre**
female sex: **sexus muliebris**
female sex organ: **vagina**
femur bone: **os femoris**
fennel: **foeniculum**
fever: **febris**
fever attack: **aggressus febris**
fever continuing: **durante febre** or **febre durante**
feverish: **febrilis** or **febriculosus**
feverish heat: **ardor febrilis**
field: **arvensis**
fierce: **ferox**
fig: **carica** or **ficus**
filbert: **avellana** or **avella** or **corylus**
filbert tree: **corylus maxima**
filter: **filtrum**
filthy: **stercoreus**
finger: **digitus**
finger's breadth: **transversum digitum**
fingernail: **unguiculus**
fingers and toes: **digitatus**
fir tree: **abies**
fire: **ignis**
first: **primus**
first name: **praenomen**
fish: **piscis**
fish gill: **branchia**
fish hook: **hamus**
fist: **pugnus**
flame: **flamma** or **ardor**
flask: **lagena**
flatulence: **flatus**
flavored: **saporatus**

flaxseed: **linum**
flea: **pulex**
fleabane: **erigeron**
flesh: **caro** or **carnis**
flesh-eating: **sarcophagus**
flock: **grex**
flour: **farina**
flower: **flos**
flowery: **floridus**
flowing to: **affluxus**
fly: **musca**
foamy: **spumosus**
fodder: **farrago**
following: **sequens**
food: **cibus** or **pabulum** or **alimentum** or **pastus**
fool's parsley: **aethusa cynapium**
foot: **pes**
foot bath: **pediluvium**
for: **pro**
for an adult: **pro adulto**
for an hour: **per horam**
for both eyes: **oculi uterque**
for each eye: **pro singulis oculis**
for example: **exempli gratia**
for external use: **ad usum externum** or **pro usu externo**
for the eyes: **pro oculis**
for the hair: **pro capillis**
for the mouth: **ori**
for the nose: **pro naso**
for the second time: **ad secundum vicem**
for the third time: **ad tertiam vicem**
for the throat: **pro jugulo**
for the winter: **hibernus**
for three days: **per triduum**
for two days: **per biduum**
forearm: **antebrachium** or **cubitum**
forefinger: **index**
forehead: **frons**
fork: **furca**
forked: **furcatus**
foul: **sordidus**
fountain: **fons** or **fontis** or **fontana**
four: **quattuor/quatuor**
four times a day: **quater in die** or **quater die**
four-footed: **quadrupes**
fox: **vulpes**
foxglove: **digitalis**
fracture: **fractura**
frankincense: **tus/thus** or **olibanum**
freak of nature: **lusus naturae**
freckle: **lentigo**
free: **liber**
free from pain: **indolentia**
frenzy: **phrenesis**
frequently: **frequenter**
fresh: **recens**
fresh water: **aqua dulcis** or **dulcis unda**
frightened: **territus**
frog: **rana**
from: **a** or **ab**
from behind: **a tergo**
from childhood: **ab incunabulis** or **ab parvulis**
from day to day: **de die in diem** or **diem ex die** or **in dies** or **indies**
from head to heel: **a capite ad calcem**
from sunrise to sunset: **a solis ortu usque ad occasum**

from that day: **a die**
from the beginning: **ab initio**
from the cradle: **ab incunabulis**
from the date: **a datu** or **a die**
from the first: **a primo**
from the inside: **ab intra**
from the outside: **ab extra**
from the side: **a latere**
from the start: **ab initio**
from top to bottom: **a capite ad calcem**
front: **frontis**
front part: **anterior**
frozen: **gelatus** or **congelatus**
fruit: **fructus** or **frux**
fruit-bearing: **pomifer**
fruitless: **infructuosus**
full: **plenus**
full of worms: **vermiculatus**
fuller's earth: **terra cimolia**
fully: **ad plenum**
fumigation: **suffumigatio** or **suffitus**
funnel: **infundibulum**
furnace: **fornax**

G

gallipot: **narthecium**
gallon: **congius**
gallstone: **chololithus**
ganja: **cannabis indica**
garden: **hortus**
garden hemlock: **aethusa cynapium**
gargle: **gargarisma**
garlic: **allium/alium**
gas: **gas** or **gasum**
gasoline: **benzinum**
gasp: **singultus**
gauze: **carbasus**
gelatin: **gelatinum** or **gelatum**
gentle: **lenis**
gentle respiration: **spiritus lenis**
genuine: **verus**
gift: **donum**
gin: **spiritus juniperi**
ginger: **zingiber**
girdle: **zona**
girl: **puella**
give: **da**
glass: **vitrum**
glass rod: **virga vitrea**
gloomy: **tenebrosus**
glowing: **luminosus**
goat's milk: **lac caprae**
gold: **aurum**
gold leaf: **aurum foliatum** or **lamina auri**
golden: **aureus**
golden seal: **hydrastis**
goldfish: **hippurus**
good: **bonus** or **bene**
good for everything: **panchrestus**
goose bumps: **cutis anserina**
goose grease: **adeps auserinus**
gooseberry: **ribes grossularia**
gourd: **cucurbita**
gout: **dolor artuum**
gradually: **gradatim**
grain: **granum**
granulated: **granulatus**
grape: **uva**
grapes (Corinthian): **uvae Corinthae** or **uvae Corinthiacae**
grapevine: **vitis**
grass: **gramen** or **herba**
grasshopper: **gryllus**

grassy: **gramineus**
grease: **pinguedo**
great: **magnus**
greater: **major**
greatest: **maximus**
green: **viridis**
grey hair: **canities**
grind: **frendere**
grinding of the teeth: **brygmus**
gristle: **cartilago**
groin: **inguen**
gruel: **jusculum avenaceum**
guest: **hospes** or **hospita**
gum: **gummi**
gum arabic: **acacia** or **acaciae gummi** or **gummi Arabicum**
gum-bearing: **gummifer** or **cummiphorus**
gums: **gingiva**
gurgling intestines: **bombus**
guts: **viscera**
gymnastic: **gymnasticus**

H

hair: **capillus** or **crinis** or **pilus**
hair lotion: **lotio crinalis**
hair of head: **coma**
hairy: **comans** or **comatus** or **hirsutus** or **pilosus**
half: **semis**
half a pound: **selibra**
half an hour: **semihora**
half an ounce: **semuncia**
half-dead: **semivivus** or **seminex**
half-naked: **seminudus**
halibut: **hippoglossus**
hallucinations: **aegri somnia**
hand: **manus**
handful: **manipulus**
happy: **felix**
hard: **durus**
hard skin: **callus** or **callosus**
hardened: **duratus**
harmless: **innoxius**
hartshorn: **cornu cervi**
hastily: **festinato**
having thorns or spines: **acanthus**
hazelnut: **corylus avellana**
head: **caput**
head bandage: **galea**
headache: **cephalagia**
headless: **acephalus**
healing: **cura** or **curatio**
healing power: **vis medicatrix**
health: **valetudo**
healthful: **salutaris**
healthy: **sanus**
heart: **cor**
heart palpitation: **tremor cordis**
heart-shaped: **cordatus**
heartbeat: **pulsus cordis**
heartburn: **ardor ventriculi**
heartsick physically: **animo aeger**
heat: **aestus**
heat from a flame: **ardor**
hedgehog: **echinus**
heel: **calx** or **calcaneum**
hellebore: **veratrum**
helping: **adjuvans**
hemlock: **conium**
hen: **gallina**
henbane: **hyoscyamus**
herb: **herba**
herd: **grex**
here and there: **passim**
here lies buried: **hic sepultus est**
hereafter: **abhinc**
hermaphrodite: **hermaphroditus**

I

in still waters: **in aquis quietis**
in the back: **in dorso**
in the first place: **imprimis**
in the manner directed: **more dicto**
in the manner prescribed: **ex modo praescripto**
in the throat: **in fauces**
in the usual manner: **more solito**
in the womb: **in utero**
in this place: **hoc loco**
in two doses: **ad duas vices**
in water: **ex aqua**
in what manner: **quomodo**
incense: **tus/thus**
incisors: **dentes incisores**
incurable: **insanabilis**
index finger: **digitus index**
India rubber: **caoutchouc**
Indian corn: **mays**
Indian tobacco: **lobelia inflata (lobelia)**
inedible: **inedulis**
infant: **infans**
infested: **infestus**
inflammation: **inflammatio**
infusion: **infusio** or **infusum**
inhalation: **inhalatio**
injection: **injectio**
injury: **injuria** or **vulnus**
insane: **amens** or **insanus**
insanity: **insania** or **dementia**
inside: **intra**
instantly: **instanter**
intermittent fever: **anetus**
internal: **internus**
interrupted intercourse: **coitus interruptus**
intestinal: **intestinalis** or **entericus**
intestines: **intestinum**
into each ear: **in singulas aures**
into the left ear: **in aurem sinistram**
into the left eye: **in oculum sinistrum**
into the right ear: **in aurem dextram**
into the right eye: **in oculum dextrum**
intoxicated: **temulentus**
intramuscular: **intramuscularis**
iodine: **iodinium** or **iodum**
iodized: **iodatus**
Irish moss: **chondrus crispus**
iron: **ferrum**
it does not hurt: **non dolet**
it does not melt: **non liquet**
it is not permitted: **non licet**
itch: **prurigo** or **psora**
itching: **pruriens** or **pruritus**
ivory: **ebur**
ivy: **hedera**

J

jaborandi: **pilocarpus**
jar: **amphora** or **olla**
jaundice: **icterus**
jaundiced: **ictericus**
jaw: **mala** or **maxilla**
jet of water: **aqua saliens**
joint: **articulus**
joint pain: **articulorum dolor**
joints: **artuum**
juice: **sucus/succus**
juiceless: **exsucidus**
juicy: **sucidus**
julep: **julepus** or **julapium**
juniper: **juniperus**

K

keratin: **keratinum**
kidneys: **renes**
kiss: **osculum**
knee: **genu**
kneecap: **geniculum** or **patella**
knocked knees: **genua valga**
knot: **nodus**
knotty: **genticulatus**:
knuckle: **articulus**
kola nut: **cola**

L

label: **titulus**
label it thus: **signetur**
lack of sensation: **torpor**
lactated: **lactatus**
lactic acid: **acidum lacticum**
lactose: **lactosum**
lameness: **clauditas**
lanolin: **lanolinum** or **adeps lanae**
larch tree: **larix**
lard: **axungia** or **adeps** or **lardum** or **laridum** or **pinguedo**
large (capacity): **amplus**
large (size): **magnus**
larkspur seed: **delphinium**
last: **ultimus**
last month: **ultimo** or **ultimo mense**
late: **tardus** or **serus**
late at night: **sera nocte**
latticed: **clathratus**
lavender: **lavandula**
law: **lex**
laxative: **laxans** or **laxativus** or **alviducus/alviducum** or **aperiens**
layer upon layer: **stratum super stratum**
lead: **plumbum**
leaf: **folium**
leafless: **infrons**
leather: **aluta**
leech: **hirudo**
left: **laevus** or **sinister**
left armpit: **ala laeva**
left ear: **auris laeva**
left eye: **oculus sinister**
left side: **sinistra**
left wing: **ala laeva**
leg: **crus**
lemon: **citrus limonium** (**limon**) or **malum medicum** or **malum citrium**
lemon balm: **melissa officinalis**
lemon juice: **succus limonis**
lemon peel: **cortex limonis**
less: **minus**
let blood be drawn: **mittatur sanguis**
let it be applied: **applicetur**
let it be boiled: **coquatur**
let it be coated: **tunicetur**
let it be continued: **perstetur**
let it be divided: **dividatur**
let it be given: **detur**
let it be made: **fiat**
let it be repeated: **repetatur** or **iteretur**
let it be rubbed: **perfricetur**
let it be rubbed in: **infricetur**
let it be sent: **mittatur**
let it be swallowed: **deglutiatur**
let it be taken: **sumatur**
let it stand: **stet**
let them be mixed: **misceantur**
let them be taken: **sumantur**

let there be added: **adde**
lettuce: **lactuca**
library: **bibliotheca**
licorice: **glycyrrhiza**
life: **vita**
life force: **vis vitae** or **vis vitalis**
life principle: **aura vitalis** or **animus**
life-sustaining: **supersubstantialis**
lifeless: **inanimus**
lifelike: **ad vivum**
light: **lux** or **lumen**
light (in weight): **levis** or **laevis**
lily of the valley: **convallaria**
limb: **membrum**
limb by limb: **membratim**
lime: **calx**
lime (fruit): **limetta**
lime juice: **succus limettae**
lime water: **aqua calcis**
linen: **linteum** or **linteola**
liniment: **linimentum**
linseed: **linum**
lion tooth: **dens leonis**
lip: **labium**
lip muscle: **orbicularis oris**
lips: **labia**
liquid: **liquidum**
liquified: **liquefactus**
listless spirit: **remisso animo**
literally: **verbatim**
little: **paucus** or **pauculum**
little by little: **paulatim**
lively: **vividus**
liver: **iecur/jecur** or **hepar**
living: **vivus**:
lizard: **lacerta**
locally: **localiter**
lock of hair: **cincinnus**
lockjaw: **trismus**
loin: **lumbus**
long: **longus**
long-tailed: **longicaudatus**
loose: **laxus**
loose stools: **sedes liquidae**
loosened: **laxatus**
loss of voice: **vox abscissa**
lotion: **lotio**
louse: **pediculus**
love: **amor**
love potion: **philtrum**
lower: **inferior** or **inferus**
lower arm: **ulna**
lower back: **tergum**
lower jaw: **maxilla inferior** or **mandibula**
lowest: **infimus** or **infumus**
lowest part: **infimus** or **infumus**
lozenge: **trochiscus** or **rotula**
lucerne: **medicago**
lukewarm: **tepidus** or **subtepidus**
lunch: **prandium**
lung: **pulmo**
lying down: **cubitus** or **decubitus**

M

macerate: **macera**
madness: **insania** or **mania** or **vesania** or **rabies**
maimed: **mancus**
maize: **zea mays** (**mays**) or **maydis**
make: **fac**
male: **mas** or **masculus**
male reproductive system: **pudenda virorum**
male sex: **sexus virilis**

mix together: **commisce**
mixed: **mixtus**
mixture: **mistura**
moderation: **mediocritas**
molars: **dentes molares**
molasses: **sacchari faex** or **syrupus fuscus**
mole: **talpa**
mole (skin): **naevus/nevus**
money: **nummus**
monk's hood: **aconitum**
monkey: **simia** or **simius**
month: **mensis**
monthly: **per mensem** or **menstruus**
moon: **luna**
moonseed: **menispermum**
more: **plus**
more or less: **magis minusve**
more than usual: **supra morem**
morning: **mane**
morning and evening: **mane et vespere**
morning and night: **mane et nocte**
morphine: **morphina**
morsel: **frustum** or **mica**
mortal: **mortalis**
mortar: **mortarium**
mother: **mater**
mouse: **mus**
mouth: **os**
mouthwash: **collutorium**
muddy: **luteus**
mumps: **angina parotydea**
muscle: **musculus**
muscle spasms: **angina pectoris**
muscular: **lacertosus**
mushroom: **agaricus** or **boletus** or **fungus**
musk: **moschus**
mustard: **sinapis**
mustard plaster: **cataplasma sinapis**
mute: **mutus**
mutton suet: **adeps ovillus**
myrrh: **myrrha**
myrtle tree: **myrtus**

N

nail: **unguis** or **ungula**
naked: **nudus**
naked body: **nudatum corpus**
name: **nomen**
namely: **videlicet**
narrow: **angustus**
nasal bougie: **buginarium**
nasal douche: **collunarium**
natural: **naturalis**
navel: **umbilicus**
near: **prope**
nearest: **proximus**
neck: **collum** or **collus**
needle: **acus** or **acer**
neither sex: **neuter**
nerve: **nervus**
nest: **nidus**
nettle: **urtica**
network: **plexus**
neutral: **neutralis**
new: **novus**
new species: **species novum**
newly born: **neonatus**
next: **deinde**
next month: **proximo** or **proximo mense**

next to: **iuxta** or **juxta**
night: **nox**
night and morning: **nocte et mane**
nightingale: **luscinia**
nightshade: **solanum**
nipple: **papilla**
nitric acid: **aqua fortis**
nitrogen: **nitrogenium**
no: **non**
no more: **jam non**
node: **nodus**
non-toxic: **detoxicatus**
none: **nullus**
northern: **borealis**
nose: **nasus** or **naris**
nose drops: **naso guttae**
nostril: **naris**
nostrils: **nares**
not of sound mind: **non compos mentis**
not to repeat: **ne repetatur**
not too much: **ne nimis**
notched: **crenulatus**
note well: **nota bene**
nothing: **nihil** or **nil**
nothing by mouth: **nil per os**
nourishing: **nutriens**
nourishment: **nutrimen** or **nutrimentum** or **victus**
now: **jam**
now and then: **interdum**
number: **numerus**
numbness: **torpor**
nut: **nux**
nutgall: **galla**
nutmeg: **nux moschata** or **myristica moschata (myristica)**

O

oak: **quercus**
oat grain: **avena**
oatmeal: **farina avenae** or **avenae farina**
obscure: **obscurus** or **opacus**
obsolete: **obsoletus**
odorless: **inodorus**
odorous: **odoratus**
of the morning: **matutinus**
official: **officialis**
oil: **oleum**
oiled: **oleatus**
oily: **oleosus**
ointment: **unguentum**
old: **vetus**
old age: **geraticus** or **senectus** or **canities**
old man: **senex**
older: **senior**
olive: **oliva**
olive oil: **oleum olivae** or **olivum**
on each occasion: **toties quoties**
on the ground: **humi**
on the left: **a sinistra** or **laevo**
on the right: **a dextra**
once: **semel**
once a day: **semel in die** or **semel die**
one: **unus**
one by one: **singillatim** or **singuli**
one now, another later: **alius alias**
one thousand: **mille**
one-half: **dimidius**

onion: **allium cepa** (**cepa**)
open: **patens**
open air: **sub divo**
opened: **apertus**
opening: **aperiens** or **ostium**
optic: **opticus**
optic nerve: **ophthalmia neonatorum**
optical illusion: **deceptio visus**
orally: **per os**
orange: **citrus aurantium** (**aurantium**)
orange (color): **aurantius** or **aurantiacus**
orange-flower water: **aqua naphae**
ordinary: **ordinarius**
ounce: **uncia**
ovary: **ovarium**
ox: **bos** or **bovis**
oxidized: **oxidatus**
oxygen: **oxygenium**
oyster: **ostrea**

P

pain: **dolor** or **angina**
pain continuing: **durante dolore**
pain-relieving medicines: **anodyna**
painful: **dolens**
painful part: **partem dolentem**
painless: **sine dolore**
painted: **pictus**
palate: **palatum**
pale: **pallidus**
palm of the hand: **palma**
pancreatic: **pancreaticus**
pancreatic fluid: **liquor pancreatis**
pantry: **carnarium**
paraffin: **paraffinum**
parched: **aridus**
parent: **parens**
Parkinson's disease: **paralysis agitans**
parsley: **petroselinum**
parsnip: **pastinaca**
part: **pars**
partition: **partitio**
partly: **ex parte**
parts: **partes**
passion flower: **passiflora**
paste: **pasta**
pastry: **crustulum**
patient: **aeger** or **aegra** or **patiens**
pea: **pisum**
peach: **amygdalus persica**
peanut: **arachis**
pear: **pirus/pyrus**
pectoral: **pectoralis**
peel: **cortex**
peeled: **decorticatus**
pencil: **stylus/stilus** or **penicillum**
penis (male member): **membrum virile**
penknife: **scalprum**
pennyroyal: **mentha pulegium** (**pulegium**)
pepper: **piper**
peppermint: **mentha piperita** (**piperita**)
peppery: **piperitus**
pepsin: **pepsinum**
percolator: **percolum**
peroxide: **peroxidum**
perspiration: **sudor** or **sudatio**
pest: **pestis**

pestilence: **pestis**
pestle: **pistillum** or **pilum**
petal: **petalum**
petroleum jelly: **vaselinum** or **petrolatum**
petroleum oil: **petroleum**
pharmaceutical: **pharmaceuticus**
pharmacist: **medicamentarius**
phosphoric: **phosphoricus**
physician: **medicus**
physics: **physica**
physiological: **physiologicus**
pickled: **conditus**
pierced: **foratus** or **perforatus**
pig: **sus**
pigeon: **columba** or **columbus**
pigment: **pigmentum**
pill: **pilula** or **bolus**
pill box: **pyxis**
pimple: **papula** or **pustula**
pine: **pinus**
pineal gland: **conarium**
pint: **octarius** or **sextarius**
pipe: **fistula** or **tubus**
pistachio: **pistachium**
pit of the stomach: **anticardium** or **scrobiculo cordis** or **scrobiculus cordis**
pitch: **pix** or **bitumen**
pitch pine: **picea**
pitch-black: **piceus**
place: **locus**
plague: **lues**
plant bulb: **bulbus**
plantain: **plantago**
plaster: **emplastrum**
plastic: **ductilis**
plenty: **copia**
plucked: **carptus**
plum: **prunum**
plum tree: **prunus**
point: **punctum**
pointed: **acuminatus**
poison: **toxicum** or **venenum** or **virus**
poison ivy: **rhus radicans**
poison oak: **rhus toxicodendron**
poison tablet: **toxitabella**
poisonous: **venenosus** or **venificus** or **virosus**
poke root: **phytolacca**
pomade: **pomadum**
pomegranate: **granatum** or **malum punicum** or **punica granatum**
poor vision: **caligo lentis**
poplar tree: **populus**
poppy: **papaver**
porcupine: **herinacius**
pore: **porus**
porridge: **puls**
port wine: **vinum portense** or **portensis**
postponement: **dilatio**
postscript: **postscriptum**
potash: **potassa** or **kali**
potassium: **potassium** or **kalium**
potion: **potio** or **potus**
pottage: **puls**
pouch: **marsupium**
poultice: **cataplasma**
pour in: **infunde**
pour off: **decanta**
pour out: **effunde**
powder: **pulvis**
powdered: **pulverisatus**
power: **vis**
powerful: **potens**
premature: **praecox**

preparation: **praeparatio**
prepared: **paratus** or **praeparatus**
prescription: **praescriptio** or **praescriptum**
presence of fever: **adstante febre**
presence of mind: **praesentia animi**
present: **adstans** or **adsum**
prickly ash: **xanthoxylum**
prior: **prius**
proportion: **ratio**
prostrate: **procumbens**
protein: **proteinum**
prudence: **prudentia**
prune: **prunum**
pubescent: **pubescens**
pubic bone: **ossa pubis**
pulp: **pulpa**
pulsating: **pulsatio**
pulse: **pulsus**
pulverized: **pulveratus**
pumice: **pumex**
pumpkin: **cucurbita pepo** (**pepo**)
pure: **purus**
purgative: **purgus** or **purgativus**
purging: **purgans**
purging of the bowels: **purgatio alvi**
purified: **purificatus** or **depuratus**
purple: **purpureus**
puzzle of doctors: **crux medicorum**
pyramid-shaped: **pyramidalis**

Q

quack: **empiricus** or **pharmacopola**
quack medicine: **nostrum**
quadruple: **quadruplex**
Quaker button: **nux vomica**
quantity: **quantitas**
quart: **duo sextarii**
question: **quaestio** or **questio**
quicklime: **calx viva**
quickly: **cito**
quicksilver: **argentum vivum** or **hydrargyrum**
quince: **cydonium**
quinine: **quinina** or **chininum**

R

rag: **pannus**
rain: **pluvia**
rainwater: **aqua pluvia** or **aqua pluvialis** or **aqua caelestis**
rainwater basin: **impluvium**
raisins: **uvae passae** (**passulae**)
ram: **aries**
raspberry: **rubus idaeus**
raven: **corax**
raw: **incoctus**
rear part: **posterior**
recent: **recens**
recovery: **recuperatio**
rectal: **rectalis** or **pro recto**
red: **ruber** or **rubrum**
red cedar: **sabina**
red currant: **ribes rubrum**
red pepper: **capsicum**
red wine: **vinum rubrum**
reddish: **rufus** or **russus**
reduced: **redactus** or **reductus**
refined: **rectificatus**
refined sugar (refined): **saccharum purificatum**
relish: **pulmentum**

remainder: **reliquum** or **reliquus**
remedy: **remedium**
repeatedly: **toties quoties** or **identidem**
residue: **residuum**
resin: **resina**
rest: **quies**
restless: **inquietus**
resuscitated: **redivivus**
rheumatic: **rheumaticus**
rhubarb: **reubarbarum/ rheubarbarum**
rib: **costa**
ribbed: **costatus**
rice: **oryza**
Rigg's disease: **pyorrhea alveolaris**
right: **dexter**
right armpit: **ala dextra**
right ear: **auris dextra**
right eye: **oculus dexter**
right hand: **dextra** or **dextera**
right wing: **ala dextra**
rind: **cortex**
ring finger: **digitus anularius**
ringing in the ears: **tinnitus aurium** (**tinnitus**)
ringworm: **herpes circinatus**
ringworm of the scalp: **tinea capitis** or **porrigo**
ripe: **maturus**
river water: **aqua fluvialis**
roasted: **torrefactus**
rock: **petra**
rock salt: **sal gemmae**
rod: **virga**
root: **radix**
rope: **funis**
rose: **rosa**
rosemary: **rosmarinus**
rotten: **putridus** or **putris**
rounded: **circinatus**
rub: **tere**
rub together: **tere simul**
rub well: **tere bene**
rubbed: **tritus**
rubber: **elastica**
rubbing: **fricamentus**
rum: **spiritus sacchari**
rupture: **hernia**
rust: **ferrugo**
rye: **secale**

S

sac: **bursa** or **diverticulum**
saccharin: **glusidum**
sack: **saccus** or **sacculus**
sad: **tristis**
safety: **salus**
sage: **salvia**
said: **dictus**
sainted: **sanctus**
sallow: **pallidus**
salt: **sal**
saltwater bath: **balneum maris**
salty water: **aqua salsa**
salve mull: **mulla**
sample: **specimen**
sand: **arena**
sand bath: **balneum arenae**
sandalwood: **santalum**
sane: **sanus**
sanity: **sanitas**
sarsaparilla: **sarza** or **smilax**
saturated: **saturatus**
sauna: **sudatorius**
saw: **serra**
saw palmetto: **sabal**
scales: **lamina**

scalloped: **crenulatus**
scalp: **cutis capitis** or **epicranium**
scalpel: **scalpellum**
scaly: **squamatus**
scar: **cicatrix**
scarlet: **coccineus**
scarlet fever: **scarlatina**
scissors: **forfex**
scorpion: **scorpio** or **nepa**
scraped: **rasuratus**
scraped off: **abrasus**
sculpted: **sculptus**
scurvy: **scorbutus**
sea: **mare**
seasickness: **nausea marina**
seasoning: **condimentum**
seawater: **aqua marina**
seaweed: **alga** or **fucus**
second: **secundus**
second self: **alter ego**
secret: **arcanum**
sedating: **sedativus**
sedative: **sedans**
seed: **semen**
seized: **captus**
send: **mitte**
send such: **mitte tales**
senile: **senilis**
sense of smell: **olfactus**
separately: **separatim**
septic: **septicus**
serpent: **serpens** or **anguis**
serrated: **serratus**
sesame: **sesamum**
severe sore throat: **angina maligna**
sex: **sexus**
sex organs: **naturalia**
sexual intercourse: **coitus**
shade: **umbra**
shaded: **opacus**
shadow: **umbra**
shady: **umbrosus** or **opacus**
shaggy: **villosus**
shake: **agita**
shake before dispensing: **agita ante dispensationem**
shaken: **concussus**
shaking palsy: **synclonus ballismus**
sharp: **acer** or **acutus**
shaved: **rasus**
sheep: **ovis**
shell: **testa**
sherry: **vinum xericum** or **xericus**
shield: **scutum**
shield fern: **aspidium**
shinbone: **tibia** or **crus**
shingles: **herpes zoster**
short: **brevis**
short-tailed: **brevicaudatus**
shoulder: **humerus/umerus**
shoulder blade: **scapula** or **armus**
sick: **aeger** or **aegra**
sick man: **aegrotus**
sick woman: **aegrota**
sickness: **infirmitas** or **languor**
side: **latus**
sieve: **colum** or **cribrum**
sigh: **suspirium**
sign: **signum**
signature: **signatura** or **subscriptum**
silk: **sericum**
silken: **sericus**
silver: **argentum**
silvery: **argenteus**
similar: **similis**

simple: **simplex**
sinew: **nervus**
single: **singulus**
singular: **singularis**
sister: **soror**
skeletal system: **ossium compages**
skill: **ars**
skilled: **peritus**
skimmed: **despumatus**
skin: **cutis** or **derma** or **pellis**
skin rash: **erythema**
skull: **calvaria**
skullcap: **scutellaria**
sleep: **somnus**
sleep inducing: **somniferus** or **sopiens** or **soporiferus**
sleepless: **ex somnis** or **insomnis**
sleeplessness: **insomnitas** or **vigilia**
sleepy: **somnolentus**
slender: **junceus**
slight fever: **febricula**
slippery: **lubricus**
slippery elm: **ulmus fulva**
slow: **tardus**
small: **parvus**
small bandage: **fasciola**
small bottle: **ampulla**
small lozenge: **pastillum** or **pastillus**
small mouth or opening: **osculum**
small vessel: **vasculum**
smaller: **minor**
smallest: **minimus**
smallpox: **variola**
smell: **odor**
smelling salts: **sal volatile**
smoke: **fumus**
smooth: **levis** or **laevis**
snail: **cochlea/coclea**
snake: **serpens** or **anguis**
snake venom: **venenum** or **lachesis**
sneezeweed: **helenium**
sneezing: **sternutatio**
snoring: **stertor**
snout: **rostrum**
snow: **nix**
snow water: **aqua nivalis**
snowy white: **nivalis** or **niveus**
snuff: **sternutatorium** or **sternutamentum**
soap: **sapo**
soap tree: **quillaja saponaria (quillaja)**
soapy: **saponarius**
sociable: **gregarius**
soda: **nitrum**
sodium: **natrium**
soft: **mollis**
softening: **emolliens**
softening of the bones: **mollities ossium**
softening of the brain: **mollities cerebri**
solar: **solaris**
solar plexus: **centrum commune**
sole of the foot: **planta**
solid: **solidus**
soluble: **solubilis**
solution: **solutio** or **solutum**
son: **filius**
soon: **mox**
soothing: **demulcens**
sore: **ulcus**
sorrel: **rumex**
sound: **sonus**
sound of mind: **compos mentis**

soundness: **salubritas**
soup: **jus** or **jusculum**
sour: **acerbus**
sourness: **acerbitas** or **acidulus**
southern: **australis**
sovereign remedy: **remedium efficacissimum**
sow: **porca**
space: **spatium**
spatula: **rudicula**
spearmint: **mentha viridis**
speech impediment: **haesitantia linguae**
sperm duct: **vas deferens**
spermaceti: **cetaceum**
spider: **aranea**
spiked: **spicatus**
spinal column: **columna vertebralis**
spinal cord: **medulla spinalis**
spine: **spina**
spiny: **echinatus**
spirit: **spiritus**
spitting of blood: **haemoptysis**
spittle: **saliva** or **sputum**
spleenwort fern: **asplenium**
splinters: **ramenta**
sponge: **spongia**
spoon: **cochleare**
sports doctor: **medicus ludi**
spot: **macula**
spotless: **sine maculis**
spots before the eyes: **flocci volitantes** or **muscae volitantes**
spouse: **conjunx**
sprain: **stremma**
spray: **nebula**
spread: **extende** or **extensus**
spring: **ver**
spring water: **aqua fontana** or **aqua fontis** or **aqua fontalis**
sprinkle: **consperge**
sprout: **germen**
squared: **quadratus**
squeezed out: **expressus**
squill (sea onion): **scilla** or **urginea**
squinting: **strabismus**
St. Anthony's fire (erysipelas): **ignis sancti Antonii**
St. Ignatius' bean: **ignatia**
St. John's wort: **hypericum perforatum**
stainless: **denigrescens**
standing water: **stagnum**
star: **stella**
star anise: **illicium anisatum**
starch: **amylum**
starchy: **farinosus**
starry: **stellans**
state: **status**
steam: **vapor** or **aura**
steam bath: **balneum vaporis**
steam room: **sudatorius**
steeped: **suffusus** or **delibutus**
stem: **caulis**
stemless: **acaulis**
sterile: **sterilis**
sterilized: **sterilisatus**
sticky: **viscidus** or **glutineus** or **glutinosus**
still: **placidus**
stimulate the bowels: **ad alvum excitatandum**
stimulating: **stimulans**
stinger: **aculeus**
stinking: **foetidus**
stomach: **stomachus** or **venter** or **ventriculus**

stone: **lapis**
stool: **sedes**
stopper: **epistomium**
stoppered: **obturatus**
stored: **conditus**
storeroom: **cella**
strained: **colatus**
strainer: **colum**
strength: **vires** or **vis**
strengthened: **roboratus**
strengthening: **roborans**
streptococcic: **streptococcicus**
striped: **striatus**
strong: **fortis** or **potens**
stronger: **fortior**
stronger than wine: **fortior vino**
struck by lightning: **fulmine ictus**
strychnine: **strychnina**
styptic: **stypticus**
such doses: **tales doses**
sudden: **subitus**
suet: **sebum** or **sevum**
sufficient: **sufficiens**
sugar: **sucrosum**
sugar (cane): **saccharum**
sugarcoated: **saccharatus**
suitable: **proprius** or **idoneus**
sulfur: **sulfur** or **sulphur**
sulfuric: **sulfuricus**
sulfuric acid: **acidum sulfuricum**
sumac: **rhus**
summerlike: **aestivus**
sun: **sol**
sunburnt: **adustus**
sunflower: **helianthus**
sunstroke: **ictus solis**
supplement: **supplementum**
suppository: **suppositorium**
surface: **superficies**
surgeon: **medicus chirurgus** (**chirurgus**)
surgeon's probe: **specillum**
surgery: **chirurgia**
suture: **sutura**
sweat: **sudor** or **sudatio**
sweat-producing: **sudorificus**
sweating: **desudatio**
sweet: **dulcis**
sweet clover: **melilotus**
sweet fennel: **anethum**
sweet flag: **calamus**
sweet orange: **aurantium dulcis**
sweetened: **edulcoratus**
swelling: **tuber** or **tumor**
swine: **sus**
swinging to and fro: **oscillatio**
swollen: **obesus** or **tumidus**
swordfish: **xiphias gladius** (**xiphias**)
symptom: **symptoma** or **indicium**
syphilis: **lues venerea**
syringe: **sipho**
syrup: **syrupus/sirupus**

T

table: **tabula**
tablet: **tabella**
tail: **cauda** or **penis**
take: **cape** or **recipe** or **sume**
talc: **talcum**
taller: **eleatior**
tallow: **sebum**
tamarind: **tamarindus**
tannin-free: **detannatus**
tansy: **tanacetum**
tap water: **aqua communis**

tapeworm: **taenia** or **oxyuris vermicularis**
tar: **pix**
tart: **crustulum**
taste: **gustus** or **sapor**
tasteless: **insipidus**
tawny: **fulvus**
tea: **thea**
tea tree: **cajuputi**
tear: **lacrima**
tear ducts: **viae lachrymalis**
tears: **lacrimae**
teat: **mamma** or **mamilla** or **papilla**
teeth: **dentis**
tempered: **temperatus**
temple: **tempus**
temples: **tempora**
temporarily: **pro tempore** or **in tempus**
temporary: **temperarius**
ten: **decem**
tenth: **decimus**
tepid bath: **balneum tepidum**
testicle: **testis**
tetanus: **trismus**
tetanus spasms: **spasmus caninus**
the best: **optimus**
the cough being troublesome: **molestante tussi**
the end: **finis**
the left hand: **manus sinistra** (**sinistra**)
the loins: **lumborum**
the pain being troublesome: **molestante dolore**
the right hand: **manus dextra**
the same: **idem**
therefore: **ergo**
thermometer: **thermometrum**
thick: **crassus** or **spissus**
thickened: **inspissatus** or **spissatus**
thigh: **femur**
thin: **strigosus**
thirst: **sitis**
thirsty: **aridus**
this evening: **hoc vespere**
thorn apple: **datura**
thread: **filum**
thread worm: **ascaris vermicularis**
three: **tres**
three times (thrice): **ter**
three-cornered: **trigonalis**
three-part: **tripartitus**
three-pointed: **tricupis**
throat: **guttur** or **iugulum/jugulum**
throbbing headache: **pulsatilis**
through: **trans**
through a sieve: **per cribrum** or **trans cribrum**
thrush: **aphtha**
thumb: **digitus pollex** (**pollex**) or **hallex**
thunderstruck: **attonitus**
thus: **sic**
thyroid gland: **thyroideum**
tight: **adstrictus**
time: **tempus**
tin: **stannum**
tin (white lead): **plumbum album**
tincture: **tinctura**
tincture of opium: **laudanum**
tipsy: **temulentus**
tissue: **tela**
to be taken: **capiendus**

to fainting: **ad deliquium**
to saturation: **ad saturandum**
to taste: **ad gustum**
to the brim: **ad plenum**
to the painful parts: **ad partes dolentes**
to the painful side: **lateri dolenti**
toasted: **tostus**
tobacco: **tabacum** or **lobelia**
today: **hodie**
toe: **digitus pedis** or **pedis digitus**
toenail: **unguiculus**
together: **simul**
tomato: **lycopersicum**
tomb: **sarcophagus**
tomorrow: **cras**
tongs: **forceps**
tongue: **lingua** or **glossa**
tonic: **tonicus**
tonight: **hac nocte**
tonsillitis: **angina tonsillaris**
tonsils: **amygdalae**
tooth: **dens**
tooth decay: **caries**
tooth polish: **dens expolitor**
tooth powder: **dentifricium**
toothache: **odontalgia**
toothache drops: **odontalgicum**
top: **apex**
topaz: **chrysolithos**
towel: **sudarium**
trachea: **arteria aspera**
translucent: **translucidus**
traumatic: **traumaticus**
treacle: **sacchari faex**
tree: **arbor**
trembling: **tremulus**
triple: **triplex**
true: **verus**
trunk: **truncus**
truth: **verum**
tube: **tubus**
tuberculosis: **phthisis**
tubular: **tubulatus**
tuft of wool: **floccus**
turmeric: **curcuma**
turn: **vices**
turnip: **rapa** or **rapum**
turpentine: **terebinthina**
twenty: **viginti**
twice: **bis**
twice a day: **bis in die**
twice as much: **alterum tantum**
twilight: **crepusculum**
twin: **geminus**
twitching: **subsultus**
two: **duo**
two hours: **bihorium**
two pairs: **bis bina**
two-pronged: **bifurcus**
twofold: **duplex**

U

ulcer: **ulcus**
unaided: **sine auxilio**
unanimously: **ad unum omnes**
unborn: **nondum natus**
uncooked: **incoctus**
uncovered: **apertus**
under: **sub**
under the skin: **intercus**
undetermined: **in dubio**
undiluted: **sine aqua**
ungrateful: **ingratus**
unisexual: **dioicus**
unleavened: **azymus**
unleavened bread: **panis azymus**
unmedicated: **immedicatus**

V

W

week: **septimana** or **hebdomada**
weeping: **ploratus**
weight: **pondus**
weighted: **pensus**
weighty: **ponderosus**
well: **bene**
well-being: **salus**
welt: **vibix**
western: **occidentalis**
wheat: **triticum**
whirlpool: **gurges** or **spondylus**
whiskered: **mystus**
whiskey: **spiritus frumenti**
white: **albus** or **candidus**
white and black: **alba et atra**
white clay: **argilla**
white lead: **cerussa**
white lily: **lilium candidum**
white wine: **vinum album**
whole: **totus**
whooping cough: **pertussis** or **tussis convulsiva**
wife: **uxor** or **conjunx** or **muliebris**
wild: **ferus**
wild cherry: **prunus serotina** or **prunus virginiana**
wild ginger: **asarum**
wild poppy: **rhoeas**
willow: **salix**
window: **fenestra**
windpipe: **arteria aspera**
wine: **vinum**
wine glass: **cyathus**
wine of antimony: **vinum antimonii** or **antimonii vinum** or **vinum stibiatum**
wine spirits: **spiritus vinosus**
wing: **ala**
winged: **alatus**
winter: **hiems**
wintergreen: **gaultheria**
wisdom teeth: **dentes sapientia**
witch hazel: **hamamelis**
with food: **cum cibum**
with gentle heat: **leni calore**
with great care: **magna cum cura**
with hair unshorn: **intonsus**
with milk: **e lacte**
with proper directions: **directione propria**
with the teeth: **mordicus**
with water: **cum aqua**
with wine: **e vino**
within: **intra**
without: **sine**
without delay: **sine mora**
without dinner: **incenatus**
without exception: **ad unum**
without salt: **sine sale**
without smell: **inolens**
without stain: **sine maculis**
without water: **sine aqua**
wolf: **lupus**
wolfsbane: **aconitum napellus**
woman: **femina** or **mulier**
wood: **lignum**
wood fern: **dryopteris**
wooden: **ligneus**
wooden spoon: **rudicula**
wool: **lana**
woolen: **laneus**
word: **verbum**
worm: **vermis** or **vermiculus** or **lumbricus**
wormicidal: **anthelminticus**
wormwood: **absinthium**
worse: **peior/pejor**

worst: **pessimus**
wound: **vulnus**
wrapped: **involutum**
wrinkled: **rugosus**:
wrist: **carpus**
writer's cramp: **chorea scriptorum**
written: **scriptum**

Y

yearly: **annuus**
yeast: **fermentum** or **saccharomyces**
yellow: **flavus** or **luteus** or **xanthus**
yellow dock: **rumex**
yesterday: **heri**
yew tree: **taxus**
younger: **junior**
youth: **adolescens** or **juventus** or **juventa**
youthful: **juvenis**

Z

zebra-striped: **zebratus**
zinc: **zincum**

Printed in the United States
by Baker & Taylor Publisher Services